Positive Psychology

To Elaine, who has quietly taught me about flourishing.
(E.H.)

To Barbara, once again. Her laughter continues to be the music of my life.
(W.C.)

Positive Psychology

A Workbook for Personal Growth and Well-Being

Edward Hoffman
Yeshiva University

William C. Compton
Middle Tennessee State University

Los Angeles | London | New Delhi
Singapore | Washington DC | Melbourne

FOR INFORMATION:

SAGE Publications, Inc.
2455 Teller Road
Thousand Oaks, California 91320
E-mail: order@sagepub.com

SAGE Publications Ltd.
1 Oliver's Yard
55 City Road
London, EC1Y 1SP
United Kingdom

SAGE Publications India Pvt. Ltd.
B 1/I 1 Mohan Cooperative Industrial Area
Mathura Road, New Delhi 110 044
India

SAGE Publications Asia-Pacific Pte. Ltd.
18 Cross Street #10-10/11/12
China Square Central
Singapore 048423

Library of Congress Cataloging-in-Publication Data

Names: Hoffman, Edward, author. | Compton, William C., author.

Title: Positive psychology : a workbook for personal growth and well-being / Edward Hoffman, Yeshiva University, William C. Compton, Middle Tennessee State University.

Description: First Edition. | Thousand Oaks : SAGE Publications, [2018] | Includes bibliographical references.

Identifiers: LCCN 2018037051 | ISBN 9781544334295 (pbk. : alk. paper)

Subjects: LCSH: Positive psychology. | Self-actualization (Psychology) | Well-being.

Classification: LCC BF204.6 .H64 2018 | DDC 150.19/88—dc23 LC record available at https://lccn.loc.gov/2018037051

19 20 21 22 23 10 9 8 7 6 5 4 3 2 1

Acquisitions Editor: Lara Parra
Editorial Assistant: Leah Sorini
Content Development Editor: Emma Newsom
Production Editor: Laureen Gleason
Copy Editor: Mark Bast
Typesetter: Hurix Digital
Proofreader: Wendy Jo Dymond
Cover Designer: Candice Harman
Marketing Manager: Katherine Hepburn

CONTENTS

PREFACE

In its 20 years of existence as a new academic specialty, positive psychology has gained increasing international attention. From the outset, its focus on the scientific study of happiness and flourishing has sparked intense interest not only in the United States but also throughout the world. As simply one indicator, we have in recent years collaborated with eager researchers in countries as diverse as Brazil, Chile, China, Colombia, India, Spain, Taiwan, and Thailand. In a way, such universality of study on topics including altruism, confidant relations, life metaphors, peak experiences, and tears of joy is not surprising. It merely confirms our conviction that human beings around the world are more alike than they are different—and that our motivations and needs are, in Abraham Maslow's memorable phrase, "species-wide."

As the field of positive psychology has grown, its concepts have expanded considerably and now embrace many aspects of healthy functioning among individuals, couples, families, organizations, and larger communities. In teaching these intriguing notions based on our textbook during the past several years, we have often incorporated both classroom activities and take-home assignments to enhance students' learning. These have typically involved self-reflection as well as short interviews and guided tasks. The response to such activities has consistently been so favorable—"life changing" is a phrase we have frequently heard—that we decided to create this workbook. It is specifically designed to complement the broad chapter-by-chapter themes of our textbook, such as subjective well-being, romantic love and positive families, and well-being across the life span. To this end, we have created many enjoyable new activities and also presented "classic" interventions for flourishing that exist in the positive psychology literature, such as on gratitude and envisioning your best possible self.

The task has been a most enjoyable one. Several decades ago, we chose our career in order to help make a better world, and it seems clear that positive psychology now has this capability. For this reason, we encourage you to try these 60 activities to assist you not only in better understanding the textbook material but also in optimizing your personal growth to achieve a happier, more fulfilled, and meaningful life. If this workbook succeeds in both purposes, then our goals for it will have been achieved.

ACKNOWLEDGMENTS

For their conceptual contributions and research collaborations related to topics in this book, we are grateful to Dr. Catalina Acosta-Orozco, Tass Bey, Eric Freedman, Neeta Relwani Garg, Joseph Loftin, Jennifer González Mujica, Dr. Louis Hoffman, Dr. Susan Kaneshiro, Dr. Kuniko Muramoto, Dr. Shoji Muramoto, Dr. Fernando Ortiz, and Dr. Kirk Schneider. We extend our appreciation to several students who helped with research tasks for this book: Talia Korn, Mengzhe Li, Jonathan Mintz, and Mai Tanjitpiyanond. More broadly, thank you to the many students we have taught over the years in our positive psychology classes. They helped us to evaluate various activities for their personal impact and relevance. More broadly, we also want to thank the many positive psychologists who have studied and developed interventions over the years.

Finally, for their careful attention and enthusiasm at SAGE Publishing for this book, we are grateful to Acquisitions Editor Lara Parra, Content Development Editor Emma Newsom, Editorial Assistant Leah Sorini, and those others who have brought this book to publication.

SAGE gratefully acknowledges the contributions of the following reviewers:

Robin Belamaric, *The George Washington University*

John Gasparini, *University of Baltimore*

Julie Kuehnel, *California Lutheran University*

Caitlin O. Mahoney, *Metropolitan State University*

Rebecca E. Shepherd, *College of the Canyons*

Elizabeth Stroot, *Lakeland University*

Marie Thomas, *California State University San Marcos*

Barbara Walker, *University of Cincinnati*

ABOUT THE AUTHORS

Edward Hoffman is a leading scholar in humanistic psychology and has been writing and lecturing on topics relating to well-being, higher motivation, and spirituality for more than 30 years. He is an adjunct associate psychology professor at Yeshiva University in New York City, where he created its popular course on positive psychology. For more than 30 years, he has also maintained a private practice as a licensed clinical psychologist. He is the author of more than 15 books in psychology and related fields, including award-winning biographies of Alfred Adler and Abraham Maslow and an anthology of Maslow's unpublished papers titled *Future Visions* (Sage). Dr. Hoffman has also written several books relating Jewish thought to contemporary interests in psychology. These include *The Way of Splendor*, *The Wisdom of Maimonides*, and *The Kabbalah Reader*. A senior editor of the *Journal of Humanistic Psychology*, Dr. Hoffman received his degrees from Cornell University and the University of Michigan in Ann Arbor. He lectures widely throughout the United States and abroad, and in 2009, he served as a visiting scholar at the University of Tokyo. Dr. Hoffman lives in New York City with his wife and their two children. His hobbies include travel, swimming, and playing the flute.

William C. Compton has been passionate about well-being for over 50 years. In 1966, he began his lifelong investigations into optimal well-being in a somewhat unusual place for a future psychologist—as a Far Eastern Studies major at the University of Wisconsin-Madison. He later sought a more pragmatic approach to the study of well-being through the study of psychology. He received his doctorate in clinical psychology from George Peabody College of Vanderbilt University in 1987. He joined the psychology faculty at Middle Tennessee State University in 1989 and also maintained a private practice in psychotherapy. In 1992, Compton created a course on the psychology of well-being, at that time one of the only courses of its kind offered in colleges and universities around the world. Six years later, Martin E. P. Seligman and others placed much of the same material offered in this course under a new research heading called positive psychology. Throughout his career, Compton's research has focused on positive mental health, optimal well-being, and meditation. His research has appeared in many journal publications and conference presentations. Compton is also the author of *Eastern Psychology: Buddhism, Hinduism, and Taoism* (2012). Compton is now professor emeritus at Middle Tennessee State University. He has studied Zen Buddhist meditation and tai chi chuan for many years. Outside of these pursuits, he plays music, enjoys gardening, and makes time for "forest bathing."

AN INTRODUCTION TO POSITIVE PSYCHOLOGY

1 ARISTOTLE: THE VIRTUE OF FRIENDSHIP

Do you have a close friend? Can you always count that this person will be loyally by your side, or only in fair weather emotionally? Is your relationship one of unconditional trust, or do you each often withhold feelings from one other? Growing evidence from psychology and medicine indicates that your answers hold a key to optimal functioning. Nevertheless, the notion that a link exists between friendship and well-being is hardly new.

Nearly 2,500 years ago, the Greek philosopher Aristotle (1908) addressed the topic in his treatise on ethical conduct and character virtues, *Nicomachean Ethics*. In a highly influential formulation, he distinguished among three types of friendship—those based on *utility*, *pleasure*, or *virtue*. Those comprising *utility* were basically business relations, based on mutual tangible benefit like money or power. Friendships based on *pleasure* were founded on fun interests, such as attending sporting events or concerts together. For Aristotle, *virtuous* friendship was the highest of the three—involving emotional concern and compassionate care. In his view, friendship based on *virtue* has the greatest impact on human well-being in everyday life. He regarded such friendship as an important feature of the good life.

Since the advent of behavioral medicine in the mid-1970s, investigators have closely studied what is known as social support, particularly the confidant relationship because of its importance for our well-being. The range of studies has been wide: from drug abuse and depression among American and Canadian teenagers to health practices among young Mexican men. Research consistently shows that having a trusted friend with whom to share emotions reduces virtually all kinds of risky and self-destructive behavior. Studies also demonstrate that people with a confidant have better physical health—and are less likely to suffer from a variety of chronic medical problems. Such individuals also show greater emotional resilience and less vulnerability to depression. As reported by Dr. Paul Surtees and his colleagues (Surtees, Wainwright, & Khaw, 2004) in England's Strangeways Research Laboratory, there is evidence that having a confidant can add 4 to 5 years to one's life. Aristotle would probably have not been surprised to learn of such findings. In this activity, interview two people over the age of 40 who enjoy a long-term friendship (not necessarily with each other), that is, originating during college years or earlier. Your questions may include these: When and how did you first become friends? What topics do you discuss together? Do you enjoy any shared activities or hobbies? If so, what are these? In your opinion, what has kept your friendship vibrant all these years? Finally, what do you think is the secret to maintaining a long-term friendship?

Record your answers below.

Your Work: **Please use this space, and additional journal space as appropriate, for your work.**

_____

_____

_____

_____

_____

_____

_____

_____

_____

_____

_____

_____

_____

_____

_____

_____

_____

2   WILLIAM JAMES: GETTING YOUR SECOND WIND

William James ranks among the greatest thinkers in American history. Not only did he establish psychology as a scientific discipline in this country, but he is also revered as our most important philosopher. Born into a wealthy New England family, James planned in his youth to become a professional painter, but lacking artistic talent, he chose medicine instead. At Harvard University in the late 19th century, he developed America's first psychology laboratory and, later, turned his immense intellect to such topics as religious experience including prayer and mysticism, the mind–body relationship in health and sickness, and the nature of human consciousness.

In December 1906, James presented a superb speech before the American Philosophical Association at Columbia University. It was published a few weeks later in the *Philosophical Review* as "The Energies of Men" (James, 1907) and had a tremendous popular as well as professional impact. In this paper, James asserted that people often give up on tasks and projects too soon, that is, before they get their "second wind" to propel themselves across the finish line. "Our organism has stored-up reserves of energy that are ordinarily not called upon" but that exist and can be tapped effectively, James insisted (p. 5).

Usually, the second-wind phenomenon occurs without our deliberate planning or effort, but James suggested that psychology might someday discover ways to help each of us tap our stored-up energy, whether we engage in "physical work, intellectual work, moral work, or spiritual work."

In this activity, describe an experience in your life when you were feeling exhausted or drained—either mentally or physically—and then suddenly regained vitality and enthusiasm. What do you think caused your second wind to kick in? Did it involve encouragement from another person such as a family member or friend, a powerful moment of self-motivation, both of these causes, or something else entirely? If so, what? If you were teaching a skill or sport to elementary-school-age children, what advice would you give to help them tap into their second wind? What do you think is children's biggest obstacle to developing this ability? Do you think it's easier for teenagers to access their second wind? If so, why?

During the next week, record any experiences in which you felt tired or bored but then gained a second wind of energy and enthusiasm. See if you can identify what caused this phenomenon to occur.

Write your answers below.

Your Work: **Please use this space, and additional journal space as appropriate, for your work.**

A time in my life I felt really drained was spring semester of my first year of college. I made the decision to do online classes from home, after spending fall on campus. I didn't have it in me to continue paying the full price of a dorm when literally everything was online. I was feeling sad about missing out on the college experience + mad at the world for continually dealing with the pandemic. What caused me to get motivated was the decision to study abroad. I had wanted to for a long time but was intimidated by the idea. I decided that experience was what I needed to make up for my crappy first year of college. I would tell elementary school children that to gain a second wind they need something to look forward to. Some sort of reward they get through the hard work. I think their biggest challenge is their attention span, which is why it would be important to teach them that good things come to those who earn it. I do think it's easier for teenagers to get a second wind because they have a clear goal in mind and most of time they know what steps they have to take to achieve that goal.

3 ALFRED ADLER: DEVELOPING SOCIAL INTEREST

Another "grandparent" of positive psychology was Alfred Adler. Whereas William James focused on the heights of human consciousness—such as transcendental experience—Adler's attention was devoted to social life. He grew up in late-19th-century Vienna as a sickly child. Unable to participate actively in sports like many other boys of his time, he nevertheless gained popularity by helping his classmates with schoolwork and exuding a cheerful personality. By the time Adler entered medical school at the University of Vienna, he enjoyed close friendships often centering on politics, literature, and art.

As a physician and then as a psychological thinker, Adler saw our early interactions with our parents and siblings as the foundation for successful adult relationships including friendship, romantic love, marriage, and parenthood. In Adler's view, our tendency for social feeling is innate, but it must be nurtured through attentive parenting in order to flourish. In other words, social interest does not flower automatically; it must be constantly encouraged, such as through praise. Adler was a highly popular lecturer in both Europe and the United States, and he often addressed parent associations as well as professional audiences of doctors, teachers, and mental health professionals.

Once at such a gathering, Adler had been highlighting the importance of encouraging even young children to develop good social skills, and then the question-and-answer period began. A woman stood up and said, "I understand that children need adults to help them acquire social feeling. But how early should parents begin this effort?" Adler paused for a moment and smiled. "You must begin the moment the baby comes out of the womb!" he replied. "If you wait even five minutes, it's too late!" The audience roared with laughter.

In this activity, think back to your childhood and recall your first friend, that is, a boy or girl whom you chose to be with, rather than someone brought to your home by relatives. How did you first meet this child? Was it at school, in your neighborhood, or some other setting? What shared qualities, interests, or hobbies brought the two of you together? How quickly did the friendship develop, and how long did it last? Did you mainly spend time involving just the two of you together or more often as part of a small group? Keeping Adler's ideas in mind, what social skills did you develop from this friendship?

Record your answers below.

Your Work: **Please use this space, and additional journal space as appropriate, for your work.**

_____

_____

_____

_____

_____

_____

_____

_____

_____

_____

_____

_____

_____

_____

_____

_____

_____

_____

_____

_____

_____

_____

4 ROMANTICISM

Romanticism was a social and cultural movement that occurred in the Western world from the latter part of the 18th century to around the middle of the 19th century. This movement placed emphasis on individual expression, especially the deep experience of emotions. Romanticism often idealized the image of the creative artist who experienced the full range of his or her emotions in a deeply personal way. The movement was a reaction to rapid industrialization that forced people from farms and life in the country into crowded and polluted cities, places that many felt destroyed the dignity of the individual for the sake of technological progress.

The influence of romanticism was found primarily in literature, art, and music. Examples of romantic literature include the poetry of Keats and Shelley, along with novels by Goethe (*Faust*) and Victor Hugo (*Les Misérables*). In painting, romanticism can be seen in lush landscape paintings, such as those of J. M. W. Turner. The deep emotionality of Beethoven's music is a prime example of romanticism. Romanticism also changed the social sciences and politics. In fact, the precursors of humanistic psychology can be found in the romantic movement. Today, elements of post-romanticism can be seen in the "back to the land" movement that emphasizes small farms, growing wholesome food, the artisan and craft focus on handmade specialized products, and even environmentalism that urges people to live in harmony with nature.

For this activity, we would like you to live like a romantic artist for a week. Don't panic, we don't want you to write a novel or compose a symphony. However, we would like you to experience emotions as if you were a romantic artist. Begin by listing the works of art in your life that really draw strong emotions from you. For example, what are the pieces of music that often pull deep emotions from you? Look at other artistic works as well, such as movies, novels, poetry, television shows, and online videos. Remember, these emotions can be positive, nostalgic, sentimental, or even sad and tearful. The common theme, however, should be that they draw *strong* emotions from you. Please note that there is one caution as you choose emotions. Emotions that are clearly negative such as anger, resentment, jealousy, revenge, or depression should be avoided. An underlying theme of the romantic movement was that emotions should be felt deeply in order to facilitate the higher potential of being human. Emotions that are destructive and self-indulgent simply don't fit with that ideal.

For this activity, please allow yourself time at least once each day to fully immerse yourself in one work of art or experience that evokes deep and strong emotions for you. For your journal, please record and reflect on what it was like to experience emotions deeply for a week.

Your Work: **Please use this space, and additional journal space as appropriate, for your work.**

---

5 MY GREATEST SATISFACTION

For this activity, please rate yourself on which of the following gives you the most satisfaction in your life. That is, indicate how well each one helps to create in you a sense that life is good, that you are doing what feels right to you, and that you are spending your time wisely by pursuing these goals or activities or experiences. There is no need to reflect deeply on each of the options below. Often it is best to just go with your initial reaction.

MY GREATEST SATISFACTION IN LIFE COMES FROM:

1	2	3	4	5
not important to me	less important to me	neutral	more important to me	very important to me

1. Experiencing pleasurable feelings and sensations _____

2. Achievement, competition, reaching goals _____

3. Knowing that I'm following God's commandments _____ ("God" as you understand it or a Higher Power)

4. Relaxation, contentment, and freedom from stress _____

5. Embracing creativity, aesthetics, beauty _____

6. Having spiritual experiences (these may or may not be associated with a formal religion) _____

7. Close friendships and personal relationships _____

8. Being healthy with a sense of energy and vitality _____

9. Appreciating the world around me _____

10. Feeling happiness, joy, and positive emotions _____

11. Intense involvement in activities so that I lose a sense of time_____

12. Being involved in meaningful work _____

13. Being of service to other people or my community _____

14. Resolution of internal psychological conflicts _____

15. Having a sense of maturity, wisdom, and intellectual understanding _____

16. Having enough money to buy what I want _____

17. Being famous, being a celebrity _____

18. Being physically beautiful and attractive _____

19. Feeling an inner sense of peace _____

20. Feeling love from close family relationships _____

21. Other _____

After you complete the ratings, then please list your top five sources of satisfaction. Remember that in the pursuit of well-being we need to make choices in order to focus our attention on what is really important to us. Therefore, you really do need to choose your top five.

Your top five choices:

1. _____

2. _____

3. _____

4. _____

5. _____

By the way, we adopted the preceding choices from a review of history; these represent the ways in which people have pursued well-being for millennia. Of course, these are all healthy ways of pursuing well-being. Please note (1) your reactions to your own rankings (what does this tell you about yourself?) and (2) which perspectives on happiness discussed in the History section of the first chapter seem to be closest to your ideals for well-being?

Your Work: **Please use this space, and additional journal space as appropriate, for your work.**

_____

_____

_____

_____

_____

_____

_____

_____

FOUNDATIONS

Emotions, Motivation, and the
Nature of Well-Being

2

6 | USE YOUR STRENGTHS

This activity helps you to identify some of your strengths, virtues, skills, talents, and positive personality traits so that you can apply them to areas of life that you care about. Activities that ask people to use their strengths or positive traits were among the first interventions to be associated with positive psychology. The theory behind such activities is that most people attempt to improve their lives by trying to fix what is "wrong" with them. That is, people find their flaws and then try to change them. Instead, strength-based activities identify what you do right by finding your unique strengths and virtues and using them more often (Peterson & Park, 2009).

> **Step 1:** Identify your strengths and virtues. Here's what to do: Go to www.viacharacter .org and click on "Take the Free VIA Survey" (link on the left side of the page). You will be asked to register, but the basic VIA assessment is free. Next choose the adult version, verify you are a real person, and begin the VIA Survey of Character. Don't spend too much time on each question, just answer with your initial reaction to the question. There are 120 questions, so it will take about 15 to 20 minutes. When you're finished, you should get a list of at least your top five strengths.

> **Step 2:** If you feel some of your unique strengths were not on the list, then add those strengths and virtues to your list of strengths.

> **Step 3:** The instructions for the classic version of the strengths activity are to identify your top five strengths and for the next week "use them in new and different ways." In other words, deliberately use your top five strengths, but use them in ways that are not part of your normal routine. For example, if one of your strengths is kindness and you normally apply it only to your friends, then try to be kind to a stranger.

However, there is another way to work with your strengths. When Aristotle proposed his theory of well-being over 2,300 years ago, he listed particular virtues or strengths that he believed created eudaimonia and wisdom. However, Aristotle insisted that *all* the virtues or strengths were important and that *they all* had to be developed. Because Aristotle was one of the smartest men who ever lived, let's use his ideas for this activity. Therefore, another option is to look at your top five strengths from the VIA Survey and look at the list of 24 strengths evaluated on the VIA and use strengths that were *not* in your top five.

Step 4: For your journal, please keep a daily record of what you did and how you felt. Record your reactions to this activity, such as difficulty versus ease of applying your strengths, emotions experienced, and change in perspective and well-being. How did the activity impact other people in your life?

See the following journal article for research on strengths: Seligman, Rashid, and Parks (2006).

Your Work: **Please use this space, and additional journal space as appropriate, for your work.**

Day 1: Used humor to make friends at a club I joined and it worked! I'm usually shy and just make jokes around my friends.   Day 2: I used social intelligence when listening to a girl continually talk about herself. I wanted to cut her off and bring up a different topic but I realized she may not have any one else to vent to.   Day 3: I was curious about exploring the area around me because I'm still new. I got out of my comfort zone and drove around. I now have a much better sense of where I am and where I'm going.   Day 4: I appreciated beauty by going to a nice park, sitting on a bench, and reading. While I was there I enjoyed the sun on my face, watching the clouds go by, seeing people walking with their families and dogs. And I called both sets of grandparents because I miss them. It felt nice to relax and enjoy the world around me.

7 | SELF-ACCEPTANCE

When people evaluate their lives in terms of satisfaction or happiness, they often compare themselves with other people. Many people have the mistaken impression that other people don't have problems, they are always happy, or their lives are totally fulfilling at all times. A common consequence of making these unrealistic comparisons with others is that people blame themselves for not living the ceaselessly wonderful life they imagine others live. Trust us when we say that everyone has problems, everyone has bad days, and everyone has difficulties in life that are challenging. On the other hand, self-acceptance is simply recognizing who you are with all your quirks and idiosyncrasies and then stopping being so hard on yourself.

You may wonder what this has to do with happiness. Actually, the path to self-acceptance is very important to happiness because we can't be authentically happy unless we allow ourselves to accept ourselves. Otherwise, we put on a "happy face" partially so we can hide our unacceptable parts from ourselves and from others. The path toward self-acceptance may actually lead through self-compassion. The activity presented here come from the website of Dr. Kristin Neff who has focused her research on self-compassion (http://self-compassion .org). If you wish to explore this area further, please take a look at her work. This particular activity is called the "Letter to an Imaginary Friend." It works like this:

Think about an imaginary friend who unconditionally loves you and who is accepting, kind, and compassionate. Imagine that this friend can see all your strengths and all your weaknesses. Reflect on what this friend feels toward you and how you are loved and accepted exactly as you are, with all your very human imperfections. This friend recognizes the limits of human nature and is kind and forgiving toward you. In his or her great wisdom this friend understands your life history and the millions of things that have happened in your life to create you as you are in this moment.

Write a letter to yourself from the perspective of this imaginary friend. What would this friend say to you about your flaws from the perspective of unlimited compassion? How would this friend convey the deep compassion he or she feels for you, especially for the pain you feel when you judge yourself harshly? What would this friend write in order to remind you that you are only human, that all people have both strengths and weaknesses? And if you think this friend would suggest possible changes you should make, how would these suggestions embody feelings of unconditional understanding and compassion? As you write to yourself from the perspective of this imaginary friend, try to infuse your letter with a strong sense of his or her acceptance, kindness, caring, and desire for your health and happiness.

After writing the letter, put it down for a little while. Then come back and read it again, really letting the words sink in. Feel the compassion as it pours into you, soothing and comforting you like a cool breeze on a hot day. Know that love, connection, and acceptance are your birthright. To claim them you need only look within yourself.

Your Work: **Please use this space, and additional journal space as appropriate, for your work.**

_____

_____

_____

_____

_____

_____

_____

_____

_____

_____

_____

_____

_____

_____

_____

_____

_____

_____

8 EMOTIONAL INTELLIGENCE (EI)

Emotional intelligence (EI) can be defined as the ability to perceive one's emotions, assimilate emotion-related feelings, understand the information involved with those emotions, and manage one's emotions. Although research in this area is still nascent, there seems to be little doubt that the ability to understand and use our emotions wisely and creatively is related to personal and interpersonal well-being.

The model presented by Peter Salovey and John Mayer proposes five characteristics of EI (see Salovey, Mayer, Caruso, & Yoo, 2009).

1. **Knowing one's emotions.** People high in EI should be able to accurately recognize what they are feeling and to accurately express the emotion as well.

2. **Handle interpersonal relationships well.** People high in emotional intelligence should be socially competent and good at creating and maintaining effective interpersonal relationships.

3. **Use emotions to motivate oneself.** People high in EI should be able to control their emotions to help them reach goals.

4. **Recognize emotions in others.** This refers to the skills of reading what other people are feeling and being empathetic.

5. **Manage one's emotions.** This can include the ability to regulate one's moods and rebound after an emotional setback.

Salovey et al. (2009) proposed that increases in EI come from increasing particular emotional abilities and skills. Their model predicts that high EI develops from (1) the ability to perceive and express emotions, which leads to (2) skills at assimilating emotions and cognitive processing of feelings, which leads to (3) a deeper understanding of the complexities of emotions as they relate to the social world, which leads to (4) being able to regulate emotions more effectively. Learning how to enhance and develop your EI is clearly a skill that develops over time. Therefore, we can't cover the whole process in one exercise. Nonetheless, an activity in recognizing emotions can begin the process of developing your EI.

Begin this activity by writing down significant emotions throughout the day. Next refer to the feelings chart posted by Momentum Counselling Services in Dundee, Scotland: http://www.dundeecounselling.com/selfhelp/feeling-words-list.php. After looking at the chart, substitute any emotional labels from the chart that are a better fit with what you felt. Continuing to do this throughout the next week should help you label your emotions more accurately. Next, write about how your significant emotions may be a blend of more than one emotion. For example, if you were just accepted into graduate school you may feel joy, relief, pride, and even a bit of apprehension. Finally, try to better understand emotions felt by others. When talking with other people use phrases such as "How did you feel about that?" or "Tell me more about how you were feeling." You can also clarify your understanding by asking something like "So you felt _____ when that happened?" You fill in the blank with the emotion you believe the person felt and allow him or her to use an "emotion word" that fits better with personal experience. Hopefully, you will learn more about the person's emotional experience. Of course, by following these directions throughout your life, you will bolster your EI.

Your Work: Please use this space, and additional journal space as appropriate, for your work.

_____

_____

_____

_____

_____

_____

_____

_____

_____

_____

_____

_____

_____

_____

_____

_____

_____

_____

9 MOVING TOWARD YOUR GOALS

Begin by thinking about how you actually spend your time on a daily or weekly basis. In the space below, list the activities on which you spend the most time every day. These can be aspects like studying, working, socializing with friends, socializing with family members, and so on. Try to be specific so that if you are with friends, indicate whether you are with your best friends or merely acquaintances. If you are with family members, then are you spending time with your parents, siblings, children, or other relatives? Please list at least the top eight **activities** that you do the most frequently on a daily or weekly basis.

1. Study
2. Work
3. Take Care of my kid
4. Do an Activity for my kid
5. Clean
6. Cook
7. Take time to relax
8. Spend time with my dad

Next, change your focus a bit and please list two of your major **goals** for each of the below time periods. These should concern matters that you want to accomplish within the differing time periods.

Goals for the next 6 months:

1. Reduce stress
2. Get restraining order

Goals for the next year:

3. Get my boyfriend up here
4. Complete bachelors

Goals for the next 5 years:

5. Have more kids
6. Move / Masters

Goals for the next 20 years:

7. Learn French & hairstobe
8. Take Vacations

Now please list your top three **values** in life. What character traits, values, or virtues do you admire the most when you see people express or hold those values?

Duty

Loyalty

Honesty

If resources like time and money were not a consideration, what would be your highest priorities in life; what goals would you pursue?

Education

Family

World domination

Please rank **your first four activities** using the following scale.

1	2	3	4	5
not true	slightly false	neutral	true	very true

Activity number:	1	2	3	4
1. This activity is my choice versus others say I must do this.	5			
2. This activity gives me intrinsic satisfaction.	5			
3. This activity fits my values.	5			
4. By doing this activity, I'm making adequate progress toward important goals.	5			
5. I do this mostly to avoid negative consequences.	5			
6. This activity conflicts with my major goals.	1			
7. This activity helps me with my need for competence.	5			
8. This activity helps me with my need for positive relationships.	5			
9. This activity helps me with my need for autonomy.	5			

Review the information from our textbook on how the goals that people set and how they pursue those goals are related to increased well-being. You will see that the preceding questions relate to research on goals and well-being.

Finally, in your journal, please describe your reactions to this activity. Do your daily activities and ultimate goals match? Are you pursuing goals that research says will boost well-being? Are you using your time in a way that helps you meet important goals?

Your Work: **Please use this space, and additional journal space as appropriate, for your work.**

_____

_____

_____

_____

_____

_____

_____

_____

_____

_____

_____

10 | THE FAMOUS LAMP OF ALADDIN

For this activity please begin by recalling the story of Aladdin and his magic lamp. You may know the story from the highly popular animated version that was released by Disney Studios about 25 years ago. If you don't remember the story, here is a brief synopsis. The story comes from a collection of Middle Eastern folk tales titled *One Thousand and One Arabian Nights*. In this tale, Aladdin is a poor child of the streets who is tricked by a sorcerer into retrieving a magic oil lamp from an enchanted cave. When Aladdin rubs the magic lamp to clean it (in the original story, it is his mother who cleans the lamp), then a magical genie appears who will grant Aladdin three wishes.

Imagine that you have just found the famous lamp of Aladdin. The genie grants you three wishes. What would you ask for? (Sorry, you can't ask for more wishes or use any other clever trick to get more wishes.) Take your time with this task. You may want to list your three wishes and then put them aside for a day or two. Then, look at your three wishes again. Are they still the same? If not, change the list so the three reflect a more stable list of choices. When you are sure the list reflects what you really want then it is time to evaluate what is on your list.

Ask yourself questions such as these: What emotion(s) do I hope to foster with my choices? What behavior(s) do I hope to foster? What would I gain if this wish were granted that I don't have now? Can I realistically achieve this wish without the "magic" of the lamp? What would I choose if I could only have one wish granted?

Here are a few questions you might ask that could be helpful in evaluating your list of three wishes. Do your wishes reflect something to be gained by you or by other people as well? For example, if one of your wishes involved money, was it money for your needs and wants or was it money to help other people? Possibly, your wish is a combination of both. Do your wishes reflect a move toward positive emotions and behaviors more than a move away from negative emotions and behaviors? For example, a wish for greater income could be based on a desire to form a philanthropic organization to help out other people (a desire to foster a positive emotion), or it could be based on a desire to never feel anxiety about financial ruin (a desire to avoid a negative emotion). Once again, your wish may be a combination of both. What did you learn about your goals for well-being?

Your Work: **Please use this space, and additional journal space as appropriate, for your work.**

_____

_____

_____

_____

_____

_____

_____

_____

_____

_____

_____

_____

_____

_____

_____

_____

_____

_____

_____

_____

_____

_____

3　SUBJECTIVE WELL-BEING

11　DAILY DIARY ACTIVITY

For this activity, we would like you to create a diary for 5 consecutive days. The idea is to take about 5 minutes each day and write down at least three positive things in your life. For instance, it can be the good things that happened that day, what you have to be thankful for, or how you feel about the people who care about you. Put something positive in your diary every day. There are also interventions in positive psychology that involve writing to deal with negative emotions, but let's stick with the positive for this activity.

Because happiness is partially a result of how people interpret events, try to find something every day that you can interpret in a positive way. That is, find a positive way to look at what happened. Of course, at times your list of three good things will include experiences that were just simply good ones, experiences where no interpretation was necessary; these just felt good. Among the challenges of pursuing greater well-being is that our negative emotions often have a greater pull on us than our positive emotions. Negative emotions often seem to demand our attention and can yank us out of a good mood very quickly. From an evolutionary perspective, this situation makes sense. Why? Because in our evolutionary past, it was more important to notice threats as quickly as possible than to bask in pleasant feelings. Therefore, scientists believe, we evolved to be more sensitive to negative emotions that might signal a threat. However, this evolutionary tendency can be overcome with just a little practice. The idea is to start training yourself to notice the positive aspects of your life, while not ignoring the potential threats.

Many people find it helpful to do their writing about the three good things at the end of the day. You may write down your three good things just before going to bed. You may find this puts you into a good mood right before you go to sleep. It may even give you more uplifting dreams!

At the end of 5 days, review what you wrote and write a brief description of how you feel or how the activity did or didn't enhance your well-being. You may find it helpful to have a friend or relative also conduct this activity at the same time as you. Then at the end of the 5 days, you can share what you each experienced and how the activity impacted you both.

In positive psychology, this endeavor is known as the "Three Good Things" activity. To explore research on it, you can look at Seligman, Steen, Park, and Peterson (2005).

Your Work: **Please use this space, and additional journal space as appropriate, for your work.**

Day 1: 1. I'll start off strong & say I'm happy to be alive & healthy. 2. I'm grateful I can pursue a higher education & advance my career options. 3. I have my parents support & love, even though they are far away we talk all the time & stay updated in each others lives. Day 2: 1. I love how incredible the weather was today. The sun was shining & the temperature was perfect. 2. I miss my dogs but I'm excited to see them in a few weeks! 3. What would I do without Netflix. Day 3: Self love day! I appreciate my youth, my self worth, and my personality. Day 4: 1. I'm thankful I met a friend I'm already close with, it helps charlotte feel more like home. I'm proud of myself for getting 100% on my sociology quiz. 3. My family has already started making Thanksgiving plans & I'm very excited! Day 5: Wanted to get more broad for the last day. 1. I'm amazed by Earth's beauty constantly. 2. I'm grateful for the direction my life has gone. 3. I'm thankful I get to experience existence, it's quite the phenomenon.

Doing these journal entries reminds me to reflect on the good in my life, even when things aren't going well. Just because we're used to having certain experiences everyday doesn't mean we should take them for granted.

12 FORDYCE'S 14 FUNDAMENTALS OF HAPPINESS

Dr. Michael Fordyce was among the first psychologists to study happiness with the goal of creating an intervention program to help people become happier. He reviewed the research that was available at the time and summarized what he saw as the major findings. Fordyce summarized these into what he called the "14 fundamentals of happiness." He asserted that we could increase our happiness by evaluating ourselves on these fundamentals and then changing those that needed improvement. His research, and research by others, found that self-reported happiness could indeed increase if people followed these 14 fundamentals.

First, please evaluate yourself on the 14 fundamentals below.

Needs a lot of work	*Needs some work*	*OK*	*I'm doing well*	*I'm doing great*
1	2	3	4	5

_____ (1) be more active, get more exercise

_____ (2) spend more time socializing

_____ (3) be productive at meaningful work

_____ (4) get organized

_____ (5) stop worrying

_____ (6) lower your expectations and aspirations

_____ (7) think optimistically

_____ (8) orient yourself to the present, be more in the moment

_____ (9) work on a healthy personality, build healthy personality traits

_____ (10) develop an outgoing, social personality

_____ (11) be yourself, be more authentic

_____ (12) eliminate chronic negative feelings

_____ (13) develop and nurture close relationships, for these are the number one source of happiness

_____ (14) value happiness—put it first in your life

Second, please review your rankings and list the ones where you scored a 3 or lower. For the next week, try to improve at least one of your lower scores. For example, if you scored low on "think optimistically" then try to catch your pessimism and make efforts to change your thinking toward an optimistic point of view. Note that working on two or three fundamentals during the week may be helpful. However, be careful, because you don't want to take on too much at one time. Be persistent, but be gentle and kind to yourself. This is not an Olympic competition for the gold medal in happiness.

You will note that some of Fordyce's 14 fundamentals are a little daunting, such as "stop worrying." That's a pretty big task! It is really hard to completely stop worrying, and it is probably not advisable to never worry about anything. Therefore, bring your own common sense to the task. For instance, you can try to stop unnecessary worrying or try to "be yourself" more when you're with friends and people you feel comfortable with. Remember that small changes can lead to large effects. Be sure to notice the small changes.

Your Work: **Please use this space, and additional journal space as appropriate, for your work.**

_____

_____

_____

_____

_____

_____

_____

_____

_____

_____

_____

_____

_____

_____

13 NOSTALGIA

If various songs or scents easily put you into a sentimental mood, don't feel embarrassed—for positive psychology shows that nostalgia isn't merely harmless; it's actually beneficial for individual well-being. It also seems that the more emotionally healthy we are, the likelier we are to become nostalgic often.

Nostalgia hasn't always been viewed this way. The word comes from ancient Greek, combining *nostos* (to return home) and *algos* (referring to pain) and was created in 1688 by a Swiss physician who discussed it in his medical treatise. He used *nostalgia* to describe the emotional distress of Swiss soldiers stationed far from home. For centuries afterward, nostalgia had a medical, and basically abnormal, connotation linked to homesickness.

Then, in the 1950s, experts began changing their view. They no longer saw nostalgia as a type of homesickness but instead as a pleasant self-indulgence about the past. Undoubtedly, this shift related to the enormous impact of TV, whose popular shows celebrated the American Old West and traditional farm life. It's no surprise that Baby Boomers—raised on such entertaining fare—were the first generation to grow up with nostalgia as desirable.

Today, positive psychology has shed increasing light on how nostalgia strengthens mental health. A research team led by Dr. Xinyue Zhou (2008) in China found that nostalgia helped people to feel more connected with family and friends, thereby reducing feelings of loneliness. These findings were consistent with an earlier study led by Dr. Tim Wildschut (2006) at the University of Southampton in England. Both researchers asserted that people with high resilience—that is, the ability to bounce back quickly from stress—are skillful in using nostalgia to uplift their mood. Of course, overly focusing on past memories can prevent us from living fully in the present, but in moderation, nostalgia can enhance our sense of closeness to others.

In this activity, interview two people over the age of 40 who frequently listen to "oldies" pop music, such as on YouTube. For both persons, your interview may include these questions: In general, why do you like to listen to pop songs from earlier eras? Is it mainly because of the memories these songs evoke, their musical styles, or both reasons? Are particular "oldies" songs associated with specific events, such as high school graduation, a college romance, or a vacation? If so, could you give two examples of particular songs that make you feel nostalgic in a specific way? Overall, would you describe nostalgia as a happy emotion, a somewhat sad emotion, or a mixture of both—and why?

Record your interview answers below.

Your Work: **Please use this space, and additional journal space as appropriate, for your work.**

_____

_____

_____

14 EXPLANATORY STYLE

It's a truism that life is filled with ups and downs. Disappointments happen to everybody—even to the most successful people. Reacting to wonderful events is not difficult: Most of us know how to celebrate. But responding effectively to defeat and failure is a different matter. Thus, among the most important concepts in positive psychology today is that of *explanatory style*: how we interpret bad events that occur in our lives. Research shows that it has major consequences for our mental and even physical health.

A leading figure in explicating the value of an optimistic explanatory style is Dr. Martin Seligman of the University of Pennsylvania. During the mid-1980s, he studied the explanatory style of Major League Baseball (MLB) players and managers. By analyzing the public utterances reported in local newspapers, he found that "optimistic teams" performed better than their previous win–loss records would have predicted and that "pessimistic teams" actually performed worse. During the same period, his study involving the National Basketball Association (NBA) reported similar findings: There was an individual as well as a team explanatory style that could be measured—and it too predicted winning above and beyond sheer athletic ability (Seligman, 1991).

In a follow-up study, Dr. Seligman and his colleagues found that a pessimistic explanatory style was a major risk factor for physical illness. Using physical and mental health data of Harvard classmates during World War II, researchers were able to retrospectively determine that explanatory style impacted college students' later health from ages 30 to 60. Those who were pessimistic as young adults were significantly more likely to have poor health when older compared to those with a "sunny" outlook (Seligman, 1991).

In Dr. Seligman view, explanatory style comprises three distinct aspects: *Permanence*. Does one believe that the distressing situation will always exist or will be only temporary? *Pervasiveness*. Does one view the unpleasant situation as all-encompassing or specific in nature? *Personalization*. Does one blame oneself entirely for a bad event or spread the blame to others?

In this activity, describe an experience that turned out badly for you—perhaps a college course or job, a friendship or romantic fling—and for which you have often blamed yourself. Write a paragraph below about the debacle, then deliberately change your explanatory style. First, recognize by writing your new awareness that the event happened and is over; it no longer exists. Second, do so by writing about how the event involved only a portion of your life. Last, do so by writing about how it was not totally your fault by identifying a person or circumstance that was also responsible.

Your Work: **Please use this space, and additional journal space as appropriate, for your work.**

_____

_____

_____

15 TIME AFFLUENCE

"We all have all the time there is," observed Eleanor Roosevelt, America's most popular First Lady, in *You Learn by Living*. "No one can tell you how to use your time. It is yours." Published in 1960, her book of advice for youth marked an era when 2-hour workday lunches were common—and futurists worried about how Americans would use their huge anticipated leisure in coming decades. Thanks to increasing automation, most social scientists were sure that employment pressures and household drudgery would lessen greatly—allowing almost everybody a feast of recreational opportunities.

Fast-forward to today—and this prediction seem laughable. Although belief in a society with immense leisure just around the corner remained dominant for another few decades, experts eventually altered their view. Among the first social scientists to measure the problem was Dr. Leslie Perlow at Harvard University—and her term *time famine* quickly caught on professionally. Studying a team of software engineers who constantly felt they had too much to do and not enough time do it, Perlow (1999) argued that corporations were crippling their workers' productivity by putting them in "fast-paced, high-pressure, and crisis-filled" settings. More recently, psychologists Drs. Tim Kasser and Kenneth Sheldon (2009) developed the concept of *time affluence*—that is, the sense that one regularly has ample time at hand. Their research showed that even after controlling for material wealth, one's experience of time affluence was linked to greater happiness. Intriguingly, too, people who reported close relationships generally had more time affluence than others. The researchers concluded that the sense of time affluence was not only beneficial to physical health and social involvements but also to emotional well-being.

Expanding on such work, an experimental study at the Wharton School of Business found that—seemingly paradoxically—our sense of time affluence *increases* when we spend time helping others. How is this possible? In their view, it is because altruistic behavior boosts our self-esteem and self-confidence—and this development, in turn, stretches out time in our minds. Thus, we become more likely to commit to future engagements, despite our busy schedules.

To enhance your sense of time affluence, keep a journal daily for a week and note on a three-point scale (1 = very little; 2 = a moderate amount; 3 = a large amount) how time affluent you felt *before* performing a volunteer activity for a family member, friend, or your larger community and then *after* you did it. Was there usually a difference in each before-and-after score? Remember, the less you hoard your time, the more plentiful it will appear in your daily life.

Record your results below.

Your Work: **Please use this space, and additional journal space as appropriate, for your work.**

_____

_____

4 LEISURE, FLOW, MINDFULNESS, AND PEAK PERFORMANCE

16 FLOW AND OPTIMAL EXPERIENCE

For this exercise, please think of something that you do to produce flow. As you recall, flow is defined as an intense involvement in an activity. The engagement in the activity is such that you are focused on what you're doing, your attention isn't split between two or more thoughts or emotions, you're absorbed in such a way that you don't notice any unnecessary effort on your part, you're not self-absorbed or worrying about consequences, and you may lose track of time because you're so involved in what you are doing. There are myriad ways that people can experience flow. People have reported flow when reading a book they enjoy; when playing sports or competitive games; when being with really good friends, family members, or others they feel comfortable and open with; when creating works of art; or when relaxing on the beach. In fact, the activities that can produce flow are almost endless. In addition, their range is often unique to each person.

There are also degrees of intensity associated with flow. Some flow experiences are mild, such as being absorbed in a project you find interesting or a conversation with someone with whom you feel close. Others are a bit more intense and may involve more activity, such as playing a vigorous and highly competitive game or being onstage performing a dance or musical event. The creator of the flow concept, Dr. Mihalyi Csikszentmihalyi (1997), often refers to this level of intensity as one that balances high skills with high challenges, that is, as "just manageable challenges" (see Nakamura & Csikszentmihalyi, 2009). Very intense flow experiences can take on aspects of altered states of consciousness, such as a drastic alteration of one's sense of time (either slowed down or sped up) and a loss of self-awareness that is similar to some religious experiences. As you might expect, that degree of intensity is rare for most flow experiences.

During the next week, please try to significantly increase your participation in an activity that generates flow. If you do not engage in the activity very much, then you should do more of it. If you already do it frequently, you can try to intensify your experience (for example, by focusing your attention on it more deeply). You may decide to initiate something that you've never done before. The main idea is to increase your absorption in and awareness of any activities that produce mild or moderate flow. In your journal, please record how the increase in flow changed your well-being both in the short run and over the course of the week. You may also record any unanticipated activities that produced flow experiences for you.

Your Work: **Please use this space, and additional journal space as appropriate, for your work.**

_____

_____

_____

_____

_____

_____

_____

_____

_____

_____

_____

_____

_____

_____

_____

_____

_____

_____

17 MINDFULNESS: BEING MORE AWARE OF EACH MOMENT

In recent years the construct of mindfulness has generated a huge amount of research. The explosion of interest has been fueled by scientific findings that mindfulness is an effective way to enhance individual well-being in a wide variety of contexts. So what exactly is mindfulness?

The foundation of mindfulness is the ability to pay attention to what is actually happening to us in the moment, including both the world outside and our inner experiences. However, it is the quality of the attention we bring to each moment that is central to an understanding of mindfulness. The attention we bring to each moment should be open and receptive while we encounter each experience with care and discernment.

However, there are at least two quite different research traditions associated with mindfulness. The first comes from Ellen Langer (1989) and centers on both awareness and the ability to break habitual ways of thinking and responding. For Langer, new awareness brings new information, then followed by active attempts to create new categories of knowledge, new perspectives, or creative solutions. The second perspective on mindfulness comes from Buddhism (see Shapiro & Carlson, 2009). Within this tradition, mindfulness is defined as an open or receptive awareness in which attention is focused on one's ongoing immediate experience. Buddhist-inspired mindfulness adds another interesting element to the focused awareness: *attention to experience without attachment to one's experiences*. Such mindfulness involves a calm observation of one's own ongoing experiences without one's usual automatic reactions or impulses, thoughts, memories, and other experiences.

Buddhist-inspired mindfulness involves self-regulation of attention and openness to experience, along with both acceptance of and detachment from the ongoing flow of experiences. Note that in the Buddhist style of mindfulness, no suggestion exists that the information gained via increased awareness should be used in any specific way. The process is simply to be aware of ongoing experience while creating an attitude of calm detachment from the experience.

For this activity, please strive to bring more mindfulness to your experiences for the next week. Specifically, try a Buddhist-inspired style of mindfulness in which you increase awareness and resist the temptation to react in any way to the ongoing experiences of the moment. Just observe, "let go," and observe again. Here are some suggestions for how to do this: (1) You can simply take some time each day and be more aware of what is happening in your immediate environment. Be aware; look around you; take in the sights, sounds, and sensations of the moment (note: this may require that you turn off your cell phone or laptop!). (2) Throughout the day, when you notice you're lost in your thoughts—when you're "spacing out"—bring your attention back to your immediate experiences. (3) You may also set the timer on your smartphone, and when it goes off, you should bring more mindfulness to whatever you are doing. In your journal, report how the activity of bringing more mindfulness to your day has affected your well-being.

Your Work: Please use this space, and additional journal space as appropriate, for your work.

_____

_____

_____

_____

_____

_____

_____

_____

_____

_____

_____

_____

_____

_____

_____

_____

_____

_____

_____

18 SAVORING

This activity focuses on savoring. What is it? Surely, most people have at times paused in the middle of an activity to fully experience something that's pleasurable. It could be taking time to really taste an ice cream cone on a hot summer day or completely immersing yourself while listening to music. Fred Bryant and Joseph Veroff (2006) referred to such moments as *savoring*. It is an awareness of pleasure along with quite deliberate attempts to focus attention on the sensation and delight in it. In a sense, savoring is the experience of seeking to extract every nuance and association contained in the complexity of a pleasurable experience. In brief, Bryant and Veroff seem to be saying that we can do more than simply "stop and smell the roses." We can "stop and really savor the experience of the roses."

Bryant and Veroff identified four basic types of savoring. The first type they called *luxuriating*, or indulging in a sensation. The second way to savor is *marveling*, or getting lost in the wonder of a moment. The third way is called *thanksgiving*, or expressing gratitude. The last type of savoring they called *basking*, or allowing one to accept praise and congratulations. They also suggested five basic ways to enhance and promote savoring. The first is *absorption*, or allowing oneself to be immersed in the experience. Of course, it is best if a person allows enough time to really immerse in the experience. Because a person must focus on sensations, the second is *sharpening the senses*, or fixating on one sensation while blocking out others. It also helps to create a savoring experience if the sensation is complex and nuanced. For instance, most people know that what differentiates a chef-inspired gourmet dinner from an excellent wine from an ordinary meal is the complexity, variety, and subtlety of the former. The third way to promote savoring is through *memory building*. Here the idea is to do something that will help you to later recall the experience. Fourth, one can help foster savoring by *sharing with others*. Indeed, research shows that savoring is enhanced when the experience is shared with others. The fifth way to promote savoring is *self-congratulation*. The idea is to allow you to feel good about an experience and to relish in the experience.

During the next week, please try to significantly increase your savoring of activities that you enjoy. As we have suggested with the flow activity, feel free to initiate something that you've never done before. Whether doing something familiar or new, the goal is to increase your engagement with savoring activities. Please use the five ways to enhance savoring listed above to deepen your experiences. In your journal, describe how you felt during the activity and how increasing your participation in it changed your sense of well-being, both in the short run and over the course of the week.

Your Work: **Please use this space, and additional journal space as appropriate, for your work.**

This Past Sunday I went to the fair with my friends and a couple new people. I love the fair so I really wanted to work on savoring the moment. First, I used absorption.

I tried to take in each emotion I was feeling and acknowledge it as part of me. I focused on being with friends, how I felt on the rides, the enjoyment of fair food. Second, to sharpen my senses I focused on each individual thing I was doing in the moment, as to not overwhelm myself with everything going on around me. For memory building, this was easy because I've always done it, I took pictures of everything that makes me love the fair so I can look back on it and remember how I felt. To share my experience with others I literally did. We tried each other's food, rode rides together, and took turns playing games. For self-congratulation I made sure to take a moment and acknowledge my current experience. I told myself "right now you're at the fair having fun with your friends, you don't need to stress about school, or miss being home, just take the world in as it is right now".

19 MICRO-LEISURE

There's little doubt that technology has radically changed the way people think about both information and relationships. Many people have expressed concerns about the potentially detrimental effects of chronic smartphone and computer use on interpersonal relationships. In fact, a survey of college students found that increased Internet use was related to lower well-being (Schiffrin, Edelman, Falkenstern, & Stewart, 2010). Fortunately, students in this study stated that face-to-face interactions were more beneficial to their own well-being than online interactions.

Another aspect of everyday life that has been impacted by technology is leisure. A survey done by a marketing company found that Millennials were "extremely conflicted about technology's impact on their leisure time."[1] On one hand, they feel guilty about spending too much time on their smartphones, but on the other hand, they believe their smartphones enhance their leisure time. Hence, an emotional conflict exists that the marketing company called the "leisure paradox." One advantage of smartphones reported by millennials involved using them for little "breaks" in the day—moments of relaxation and fun. For instance, in the middle of the day a person could take a 2-minute break and watch funny animal videos or learn more about an intriguing potential leisure activity. Such short moments of relaxation are called "micro-leisure."

For this activity, we would like you to use micro-leisure throughout the day. Wait! Didn't we just refer to the leisure paradox as being a source of tension? Because that is true, the other part of the activity is to pay attention to when, why, and how you use your smartphone and the Internet. Do you feel driven to your phone to avoid anxiety or worry? Are you going online to distract yourself from an unpleasant emotion? Do people in your life complain about how much time you spend online? Clearly, these are examples of warning signs that indicate your use of technology is problematic. On the positive side, if your micro-leisure moments are simply little breaks in your day, then pay attention to how you feel after the micro-leisure break. Did you actually feel rested, or did it increase your anxiety or conflicts? Did your little break increase your well-being or not? For example, if your micro-leisure breaks involved searching for expensive clothes that are completely outside your budget, then you could be left feeling depressed. If you don't have a smartphone with you, then micro-leisure can be moments when you mindfully look around at your world; take a few deep, relaxing breaths; or take a leisurely stroll. The goals for the week include evaluating how you use your smartphone and the Internet, noticing what uses of micro-leisure actually enhance your well-being, and increasing your motivation to change smartphone and Internet behaviors that don't foster relaxation and positive emotions.

---

[1]https://www.slideshare.net/WeAreMRY/the-new-micro-leisure-redefining-downtime-in-a-connected-world

Your Work: **Please use this space, and additional journal space as appropriate, for your work.**

_____

_____

_____

_____

_____

_____

_____

_____

_____

_____

_____

_____

_____

_____

_____

_____

_____

_____

20 CURIOSITY

Do you have many interests or only a few? At school or work, do you soon feel bored when things become routine? Such questions center on curiosity—a personality trait gaining increasing attention in positive psychology. Historically, of course, many inventors and scientists—ranging from Marie Curie to Thomas Edison—have cited curiosity as a key force for innovation. As one of the most popular filmmakers of our time, Steven Spielberg (USC News, 1994) told an audience of graduating college students, "I do believe that the greatest quality that we can possess is curiosity, a genuine interest in the world around us.... From basic curiosity, great acts are born."

Since the early 2000s, psychologists have studied curiosity as a specific trait, and among the leaders has been Dr. Todd Kashdan of George Mason University. He (Kashdan, Rose, & Fincham, 2004) helped develop the first scientific scale to measure curiosity—and then found in an experimental study that high scorers showed greater playfulness, wit, and ability to bond emotionally with a stranger of the opposite sex than low scorers. Highly curious people also gave more attention to their assigned partners during their conversation; curiosity proved to be an asset during the early phrase of romance. More recently, Dr. Kashdan's (2013) research team also found that highly curious people were less emotionally aggressive toward their romantic partner than their less curious counterparts. Why? Presumably because they were less defensive and more open to differences of opinion.

Curiosity has been demonstrated to be beneficial cognitively. In a study led by Dr. Matthias Gruber (Gruber, Bernard, & Charan, 2014) of the University of California at Davis, participants were asked to review more than 100 trivia questions such as "What does the term *dinosaur* actually mean?" and "What Beatles single lasted longest on the charts?" Participants then rated each question as to how curious they were about the answer. Then, while the researchers scanned their brain activity using an MRI machine, participants revisited each question and waited briefly for the answer. Gruber's team found that greater interest in a question—that is, curiosity—not only predicted better memory for the answer, but a day later, the results still held. Somehow, curiosity "primed" the brain for learning and long-term memory.

In this activity, identify a country that you've never visited but about which you have been curious. Over the next week, use the Internet to learn about its history, natural environment, politics, and culture, including its music and arts. In the space below, jot down facts and topics that you find intriguing from your web explorations.

Your Work: **Please use this space, and additional journal space as appropriate, for your work.**

_____

_____

_____

5 ROMANTIC LOVE AND POSITIVE FAMILIES

21 LOVE MAPS

Drs. John and Julie Gottman are regarded by many psychologists as the world's foremost researchers on romantic relationships. Many people assume that what makes romantic relationships successful is love. Although there is little doubt that love is essential to romantic feeling, research suggests that the absolutely crucial ingredient for long-lasting intimate relationships is friendship. The concept of "love maps" is among the many influential ideas the Gottmans have developed associated with successful long-lasting relationships. A love map is the information you have collected about another person that helps you to feel closer to that individual. It is a "map" or a "guidebook" that allows you to know what makes this person unique and special.

For this activity, we would like you first to think about the people in your life you really care about, the people whom you love. This activity can be focused on romantic relationships, but you need not limit it to a romantic partner. Choose one person on whom to focus and keep a daily journal for the next week on any or all of the following:

1. What is it about this person that your care about? What do you love about her or him? What stable positive traits does he or she exhibit that you like?

2. Write as much as you can about his or her likes; desires; hopes; dreams; dislikes; pet peeves; favorite foods, movies, songs, or sports teams—or anything that contributes to making that person unique in your eyes.

3. Write about how his or her likes, dislikes, and personality traits fit with your own likes, dislikes, traits, and passions.

4. Think of the ways in which you are truly grateful for having this person in your life.

In your journal, please write on how much you appreciate what she or he has done for you, how much his or her support has meant to you. Actually, if you want to really run with this idea, it can be more meaningful to talk with the person directly and say the things you put in your journal.

If this person is someone with whom you'll be spending time in the next few days, then you can add another component to this activity. Rather than simply recalling what you find unique about this person, try asking questions about his or her likes, dislikes, and passions.

You may also think of your own likes, dislikes, and passions and ask how that person feels about yours as well. Perhaps you have even more in common than you realize!

To summarize your experience with this activity, write about (1) how you felt during it and (2) how increasing your participation in it has affected your sense of well-being.

Your Work: **Please use this space, and additional journal space as appropriate, for your work.**

_____

_____

_____

_____

_____

_____

_____

_____

_____

_____

_____

_____

_____

_____

_____

22 LOVE 2.0

Barbara Fredrickson's broaden-and-build model of positive emotions, and the subsequent studies of the theory, has been among the most influential research programs associated with the success of positive psychology. Fredrickson's (2013) later research has investigated the topic of love. Her ideas about it, though, take a somewhat unexpected direction.

When most people think about love they think of an idealized version: an overwhelming emotion that lifts the heart and spirit, makes every day look brighter, brings a "song into one's heart," and leads people to dance in the streets—or at least skip for joy. In other words, most people think of romantic love as the powerful emotion they see depicted in Hollywood movies or hear in the lyrics of most popular songs. Of course, love can be an extremely powerful emotion and a source of tremendous joy. For Fredrickson, however, the fundamentals of love are subtler, more frequent, and less dramatic.

In Fredrickson's theory of *love 2.0*, she says that love is a momentary experience of three events: a sharing of positive emotions, a reflected motive to commit to each other's mutual care, and a synchrony between the behaviors of two people (she also adds synchrony between the biochemistry of two people, but that aspect of her theory is beyond this exercise). Love requires a connection built through communication, especially eye contact. She asserts that it requires us to be physically and emotionally present, to slow down, and pay attention. For Fredrickson, love happens when we pay attention to our relationship and we feel a mutual responsiveness, a back-and-forth reverberation, and importantly, these moments *do not* need to be dramatic, life-changing experiences. In fact, she states that more often they are what she calls "micro-moments of love." Note, she is saying these micro-moments can happen at any time and potentially with anyone, including casual acquaintances or even people who are initially strangers. All that is required is a shared moment of mutual understanding, a sense of connection, and a desire to be respectful of each other.

For the activity, we would like you to pay attention to your interactions with other people for the next week and notice micro-moments of love. Okay, our wording of that assignment may seem a bit pretentious. All we are asking is for you to slow down, pay attention, and notice when a mutual connection happens between you and someone else. Most of the time that connection will be mild and brief. That's all right. Just notice it and allow yourself to feel the small change in your emotional state. Of course, you can do the same thing with people in your life whom you already love. The idea is to slow down and notice how the connection changes your emotional state.

Your Work: **Please use this space, and additional journal space as appropriate, for your work.**

Engaging in this activity throughout the week definitely affected my emotions. I felt more connected to people and happier about my relationships. I noticed things like when I agreed about something with someone, laughing with new friends, and support from my parents with everything going on in my life. When I noticed these "micro-moments of love" it made me feel like I can relate and connect with people more than I consciously realize. It is extremely easy to find something in someone else you can relate to, or laugh about, or just appreciate. I think this activity will influence my interactions with strangers more than people I already love because it makes me more comfortable with them when I notice these micromoments. It also helps ease my mind because I'm often insecure about what people think of me, or if they actually like me. So hopefully if I pick up on the micro-moments of love it will give me peace of mind about being insecure.

23   MINDING IN RELATIONSHIPS

When most people think about romantic love, their first thoughts are of passion or eros. Researchers, however, tell us that passion is only part of the story of love, albeit a very engaging and interesting part of the story. In order to find a fulfilling, satisfying, and long-lasting love, it is necessary to develop a number of other skills.

Drs. John Harvey and Julia Omarzu developed a theory of relationships they called *minding.* The basic idea is that certain ways of paying attention to our partners can have tremendous benefits for relationship satisfaction. Minding is a combination of five elements. The first element is "knowing and being known" or the desire to know and understand your partner. This is the desire to know your partner's likes, dislikes, and habits and to build a set of memories together as a couple. The second element is "attributions" or the ways we explain our partner's behavior. Satisfying relationships are more likely if we often explain our partner's action with positive attributions (for example, "She was kind to that little boy because she's a compassionate person" or "He took the time to listen to me because he cares about my feelings"), rather than with negative ones (for example, "He is too self-absorbed to listen most of the time"). The third element of minding is "acceptance and respect." This involves building empathic accuracy about your partner as well as creating opportunities for gratitude, forgiveness, and compassion. The next element of minding is "reciprocity," or the sense that benefits and responsibilities are shared equitably.

The last element is "continuity," or paying attention to the relationship over time. Continuity means that you don't wait for difficult times to begin paying attention, but you build it into the relationship on a day-to-day basis. It also relates to adaptability, flexibility, and a willingness to change over time when the situation calls for change.

For this activity, select someone who is very important to you. It need not be someone with whom you're romantically involved, but it should be someone with whom you're emotionally close. For the next week, try to increase minding when you're with this person. Try listening with greater attentiveness and concern. Try substituting positive, optimistic, and stable attributions for their behavior. Listen with more empathy and compassion. Take time to remember and share times when you both had fun together or felt very close. Also, think about the give-and-take or the balance of responsibilities in your relationship, and if it is inequitable, then do something to balance the relationship.

In your journal, keep track of how these efforts at minding affect how you feel about the relationship and how it seems the other person feels as well. What aspects of minding worked best, what aspects didn't work so well or were harder to implement, what aspects had immediate benefits, and what aspects will take longer to show results?

Your Work: **Please use this space, and additional journal space as appropriate, for your work.**

_____

_____

_____

_____

_____

_____

_____

_____

_____

_____

_____

_____

_____

_____

_____

_____

_____

_____

_____

_____

_____

_____

24 SELF-DISCLOSURE

Do you easily share your experiences and reactions or, rather, prefer to keep others at an emotional distance? How difficult is it for you to reveal your innermost joys, goals, and disappointments? Research is now clear that your answers impact your happiness, though more than 50 years ago, Dr. Sidney Jourard (1959) pioneered the concept of self-disclosure. Today, it is often termed transparency, especially in a business context. As Jourard correctly asserted, the extent to which we are able to reveal ourselves to other people has important consequences for our social relationships—and for personal well-being as well.

For example, research shows that especially for romantic relationships such as dating and marriage, men and women have greater satisfaction when self-disclosure is present—and it is linked to two different aspects: feeling that we can confide easily with our partner and feeling that our partner is emotionally open to us. Studies also indicate that spouses tend to match each another in how much they self-reveal and that cultural forces are potent. For example, Hispanic/Latino persons are generally more willing to talk about a wider range of topics—such as their preferences in music, movies, and hobbies—than their North American counterparts.

Scientific findings are consistent that self-disclosure has a beneficial and reciprocal effect. That is, when we hear someone reveal personal information about himself or herself (whether in face-to-face conversation or online) we become more forthcoming too—and that event, in turn, leads the other person to self-reveal more deeply. In precisely this way, greater friendship and emotional intimacy is forged. Does this mean that we should tell *everything* about ourselves? Of course not. As Jourard would surely have agreed, it is necessary to use sound judgment in what we choose to share with others—whether a family member, friend, or colleague. Especially when it comes to the workplace, which is often highly competitive, psychologists generally advise caution about what to divulge about our personal life.

In this activity, for the next week share something meaningful each day about yourself with at least one acquaintance. It might concern a favorite childhood game or vacation, a memorable event when you were a teenager, or a recent book or movie that moved you. Do not feel obligated to reveal highly personal matters; however, avoid such trivialities as whether you had chocolate or vanilla ice cream for dessert last night. During your self-disclosing conversations, avoid intellectualization and keep the focus on your feelings.

Record below the results of this activity.

Your Work: **Please use this space, and additional journal space as appropriate, for your work.**

_____

_____

_____

_____

_____

_____

_____

_____

_____

_____

_____

_____

_____

_____

_____

_____

_____

_____

_____

_____

_____

_____

_____

_____

25 EMPATHY

Do you easily know what others are feeling? Do people say that you're a "good listener"? Do you have the ability sometimes to experience their varying moods as your own? If so, then you are strongly empathic—and this quality has probably served you well throughout life. Why? Because positive psychology increasingly views empathy as a vital trait for well-being. Not only does research reveal that empathy is a unique "glue" for binding friendships, family ties, and romantic love, it even enhances our work achievement. Certainly, the latter finding makes sense, for without adequate empathy, we're unlikely to know what engages our coworkers, clients, or customers.

The growing scientific interest in empathy represents a big change from the earlier idea popularized by Dr. Richard Dawkins (1990) of Oxford University, that everyone is born with a dominant "selfish gene." Rather, many evolutionary scientists now argue that affiliative traits like altruism and empathy have enabled our species to survive and prosper—not competitiveness and greed. Such a view also repudiates Freud's emphasis on the primacy of human selfishness, for no baby can possibly survive without caregiving adults on a daily basis.

More than 75 years ago, Alfred Adler (1930, 1938) asserted that children's empathy must be nurtured or it remains weak. Recent research shows that he was correct: Parents who are empathic toward their children ("I see you're feeling sad. What happened today at school?") are more likely to strengthen empathy in their offspring. We also know today that empathy comprises two different but related components: cognitive and affective. Cognitive empathy is the intellectual ability to know what others are feeling, whereas affective empathy involves the capacity to experience their emotions, such as happiness or sadness. Though there is clear evidence that girls are more empathic than boys in both aspects by early childhood, both genders can strengthen this trait through diligent effort.

In this activity, write about an episode in your life when someone's empathy helped you to cope better with a stressful situation. It might have involved a friendship, a romantic relationship, a school-related difficulty, or a work issue. In what specific way did this person's empathic words or actions prove beneficial? Next, write about a time when you felt glad about something you achieved and a friend or family member responded empathically with congratulations and warmth. Did this type of empathy amplify your happiness? If so, why do you think it had this beneficial effect?

Record your answers below.

Your Work: **Please use this space, and additional journal space as appropriate, for your work.**

_____

_____

_____

6 POSITIVE HEALTH

There is an old saying that goes, "The only sure things in life are death and taxes." In today's world, however, it seems that a third inevitability can be added: namely, stress. Most of us experience time pressures, worries about the future, difficulties with other people, and many other sources of stress and frustration. Finding ways to deal with the challenges of stress is one of the most important self-regulatory skills that a person can develop. Therefore, all people need to possess a set of stress management skills that they know work well for them and fit their lifestyle.

This activity is designed to help you find some ways of coping that work for you. To begin, it helps to understand the major factors that contribute to stress. First, if our physical well-being is depleted it can make stressors more difficult to handle. If you eat unhealthy food, sleep poorly, don't exercise, smoke, or consume too much alcohol, then you put yourself at risk for greater stress. Second, how we think about events and interpret the meaning of those events is a major factor in how much stress we experience. If we tend to fear the worst, interpret life events in negative ways, and devalue our own abilities to be resilient then we put ourselves at risk for chronic stress. Suggested interventions follow directly from the assumed causes: Change your unnecessarily negative thoughts to more positive, or at least more realistic, thinking.

For this activity, we would like you to increase your use of positive coping techniques. To begin, identify at least one event that is currently stressful for you.

1. List at least three ways you could change how you cope with this stressor right now. Be as specific as possible! That is, don't just say, "I'll change my thinking," write *how* you will change your thinking (for example, from thinking "_____" to thinking "_____"). As you decide on a positive coping technique you can choose one with which you are already familiar, choose one you know about but have not tried, or look at the 101 options listed on the following website: www.ditchthelabel.org/101-ultimate-ways-chill-reduce-stress.

2. List one difficulty you may have implementing the new coping styles or strategies. That is, describe how you may find it difficult to implement the changes or how you may "self-sabotage" your efforts.

3. Write down at least one way to cope with the self-sabotage you listed in item 2.

4. Try out your new strategies for a week and write about what happened. In your journal, include how well the coping worked, what you can do differently to make it more effective, and how you will motivate and remind yourself to use positive coping more in the future.

Your Work: **Please use this space, and additional journal space as appropriate, for your work.**

_____

_____

_____

_____

_____

_____

_____

_____

_____

_____

_____

_____

_____

_____

_____

_____

27 REGRETS

Do you have any regrets in life? Seemingly, everyone does—and it's probably been this way since recorded history. The ancient Israelites regretted having fled Egypt as slaves and blamed Moses for their desert malaise. The American revolutionary spy Nathan Hale famously regretted "having but one life to give" for his new nation. And the most acclaimed business leader of our time—Steve Jobs—regretted in a final interview that he had not been closer to his four children.

Though Sigmund Freud a century ago uncovered plenty of guilt in his middle-class Viennese patients—and linked it to suppressed sexual thoughts—today psychologists view regret as a different, broader phenomenon. We can certainly have regrets without feeling guilty about our thoughts or actions. Psychological research is now converging on the notion that *what* we regret, how *often* we do so, and with what *intensity* all make a difference. These findings make intuitive sense, for not everyone is fixated on past mistakes or missed opportunities in life, whereas some people simply cannot let go.

Psychologists clearly differentiate our regrets over *actions* versus *inactions*. Regrets over actions trigger mainly "hot" emotions like anger, whereas regrets over inactions typically evoke feelings of wistfulness or gloom. Research also shows that people experience more regret in the short-term over their actions, but as they age, this attitude reverses. In other words, you are likely to find lots of folks in their 20s or 30s whose chief regrets are about foolish things they've done. In contrast, those in midlife and beyond are likelier to voice regrets on what they *did not* do—and those regrets may be more painful to bear. What is absolutely clear is that severe regret is bad for our mental and even physical health.

In this activity, think of a regret of commission, that is, something foolish you did. Give yourself time to recount it fully and identify possible reasons why you behaved in this immature, selfish, or unthinking manner. Now, with the advantage of hindsight, describe a different, positive behavior you could have done. Next, recount a persistent regret of omission that you have felt. After doing so, it is useful to make a thorough "reality check." That is, would things really have changed much in your life if you had actually performed that act, or are you just fantasizing a perfect scenario in our imperfect world—to little or no benefit?

Write your answers below.

Your Work: **Please use this space, and additional journal space as appropriate, for your work.**

_____

_____

_____

_____

28 TEARS OF JOY

Have you ever cried from happiness? Do you become dewy-eyed from particular songs or the victory of your favorite sports team? Have any romantic movies moved you to tears—such as *Titanic*, *You've Got Mail*, or *Love, Actually*? Ancient literary sources like the Bible and the Greek *Iliad* show that thousands of years ago, people cried in happiness, too. But why?

When psychology became established as a science, its founders gave little attention to positive emotions. Rather, their focus was on describing pathology and disorders. Later, behaviorist leaders like B. F. Skinner ignored the entire emotional realm for its inherently subjective nature. And still later, psychoanalysts in the 1950s cynically declared that tears of seeming joy are actually tears of sadness. In their view, nobody ever really cries in joy but only with masked emotional pain.

But times change, and positive emotions are now gaining attention for their role in contributing to individual well-being. Scientific evidence is mounting that it is not enough just to avoid feeling lonely, worried, or depressed. If you really want to flourish, you must connect meaningfully with your milieu—especially with other people. In this new light, tears of joy—involving both intense and positive feelings—comprise a fascinating area of study. Over the past few years, we have conducted international research with colleagues to better understand the causes and potential benefits of this intriguing phenomenon (see Hoffman, Neeta, & Gonzalez-Mujica, 2013).

What have we found? Our initial goal was to determine what types of situations cause people to cry in happiness. We were surprised that 18 categories emerged—including some we'd never anticipated. Most frequent were those involving familial affection like attending a wedding or graduation ceremony, the birth of a child, romantic ardor, attainment of a personal goal, or a reunion of any sort. In results that should warm the hearts of media moguls, many people also reported crying joyfully from an exhilarating movie, TV program, or book (including both fiction and nonfiction). Some even mentioned the same film, such as Frank Capra's 1946 classic *It's a Wonderful Life*.

In this activity, interview two people who have cried in joy within the past year. Your questions might include these: What event triggered this experience for you? For example, was it a wedding that you witnessed or a movie? Were others around you, or were you alone? Were your surprised by your strong emotional reaction, or not particularly so? Did the same event trigger tears of joy before in your life? Finally, did you notice any bodily sensations during the experience? If so, what were they?

Your Work: **Please use this space, and additional journal space as appropriate, for your work.**

_____

_____

_____

29 PETS

Are you a dog or cat lover, or drawn instead to birds or fish? How about such animals as hamsters, rabbits, or snakes? The list of domestic animal possibilities is long and growing. The majority of all United States households owns a pet—and in many homes, pets are loved as family members. Though Sigmund Freud and his daughter Dr. Anna Freud kept dogs, and Carl Jung walked a small pig on a leash, the psychological study of pet ownership is only now gaining momentum.

Early researchers included Dr. James Bossard (1944), who during World War II authored an upbeat article titled "The Mental Hygiene of Owning a Dog," and, later, Dr. Boris Levinson, credited as the founder of animal-assisted therapy (AAT) in the 1960s. Levinson's (1962) seminal article "The Dog as a 'Co-Therapist'" described how his dog, Jingles, helped treat a socially withdrawn boy. In follow-up work, Levinson emphasized the therapeutic value of pets for emotionally distressed children—and the field slowly expanded to include children with cognitive disabilities like autism, as well as adults with HIV, traumatic brain injury, dementia, and other major health problems. Professionals also began reporting anecdotally that pets contribute broadly to human happiness and wellness, and subsequent scientific studies have revealed such payoffs as lower blood pressure, less loneliness, and higher self-esteem.

Exactly how pet ownership is psychologically beneficial remains puzzling. However, a recent study in *Science* gives a clue. A team of Japanese researchers (Nagasaw et al., 2015) found that dogs that gazed for a long time at their owners had elevated levels of oxytocin—the brain's "pleasure hormone" associated with attachment. After receiving those gazes, the owners increased their oxytocin too. When researchers gave dogs extra oxytocin via a nasal spray, the females gazed at their owners even longer—which in turn, amplified the owners' oxytocin levels. As Dr. Evan Maclean, codirector of Duke University's Canine Cognition Center, commented on this study, "maybe dogs gaze at you because it feels good. Maybe they're hugging you with their eyes" (Hoffman, 2015).

In this activity, interview two people you know who own a pet (preferably with different kinds of pets). Your questions might include these: How and when did your pet come into your life? What aspects of your pet relationship do you most value? Does your pet make you happier or help you to be more active? Are there any aspects that you find unpleasant? Would you recommend this type of pet to other people? If so, what kinds of people (e.g., children, teens, young adults, midlife adults, older adults) would most enjoy this type of pet and why?

Record the results of your interview below.

Your Work: **Please use this space, and additional journal space as appropriate, for your work.**

The first interview I did was with my cousin, her family has a dog. They got their dog a couple years ago because the one they had since she was young passed away a few months before they got the dog they have now, Winnie. She values her time taking Winnie for walks and to the park because she's leaving soon for college and wants as much 1 on 1 time with Winnie she can get. Winnie does make her happy because she is so playful and has such a big personality. The only unpleasant part is Winnie never runs out of energy so it's hard to keep her entertained all the time. She would reccomend getting a dog, dogs have such varying personalities you can find one perfect for yourself at any age. For interview I talked to my roommate who owns a cat, Mooch. He got Mooch after moving to college because he wanted a companion to keep him company. He values how independent Mooch is so it's easy to take care of her, but she is still very lovable. Mooch makes him happier because of her "adorable personality". The only "unpleasant" aspect is Mooch is super shy around new people. He reccomends owning a cat to people of all ages because they're so easy to take care of.

30 | DAILY HASSLES

You don't need to be a psychologist to know that stress is harmful for people, both mentally and physically. As far back as the 1970s, researchers have found that traumatic life events—such as bankruptcy, job termination, and divorce—have adverse health consequences. More surprisingly, perhaps, subsequent investigations revealed that major joyful events—like school graduation, marriage, or the birth of a child—also predicted physical health problems, presumably because these bring huge changes to one's customary routines. But an entirely different line of study—known as that of "daily hassles"—shows that seemingly little annoyances also exert a big impact on our well-being.

For example, Dr. Carolyn Aldwin (Aldwin, Jeong, Igarashi, Choun, & Spiro, 2014) at Oregon State University led an influential, 20-year study involving older men. Her research team found that those experiencing a high level of daily hassles were at an increased risk of dying early—just as if they had experienced such devastating life events as the death of a loved one. "It's not the number of hassles that does you in," Aldwin commented in her research paper, "it's the perception of them being a big deal that causes problems. Taking things in stride may protect you."

Several studies concerning family hassles have been conducted by researchers at Louisiana State University (see Nesteruk & Garrison, 2009; Rollins, Garrison, & Pierce, 2009). Surveying a sample of (predominantly married) mothers, the first study found that caregiving to children absorbed the most time and energy, whereas dealing with outside home repairs consumed the least. Many mothers related that the same events were often both stressful *and* uplifting. In the second study, mothers and fathers reported that the most intense daily hassles involved financial matters, household chores, child care or school-related matters, and transportation; except for household chores, mothers and fathers regarded the hassles positively. So, when it comes to family responsibilities, we're likely to find a "silver lining" to most mundane activities—and that's surely a good thing.

In this activity, keep a journal for a week to identify your daily hassles. Each day at 12 noon, 5:00 p.m., and 9:00 p.m., take a few minutes and briefly describe each hassle you experienced since your last data entry. Then indicate on a 3-point scale the intensity of the hassle in terms of your annoyance (1 = mild; 2 = moderate; 3 = strong). For example, a typical entry might be *Waited on a long line at the post office = 2*; *Filled up car tank with gasoline = 1*. By week's end, you will have developed a useful chart about what is bothersome for you. Then strategize how you can reduce these hassles in terms of number and/or intensity. Because it is difficult for most people to be wholly objective in such matters, it might be useful to show your list to a friend and elicit advice.

In the space below, present your chart.

Your Work: **Please use this space, and additional journal space as appropriate, for your work.**

_____

_____

EXCELLENCE, AESTHETICS, CREATIVITY, AND GENIUS

31 RESTORATIVE NATURE

More than a century ago, the influential naturalist-explorer John Muir (1912/2014) declared that "everybody needs beauty . . . places . . . where nature may heal and cheer, and give strength to the body and soul alike." Having inspired President Theodore Roosevelt and Congress to create the national parks system, Muir had an ardent belief in nature's beneficial effect on the human psyche. Now, more than a century after his death in 1914, researchers are increasingly recognizing the accuracy of his insights.

For example, an international team led by Dr. Terry Hartig at Uppsala University has been studying psychological restoration, that is, the sense of renewed vitality, strength, and even hope that immersion in nature can provide. A variety of individual benefits have been found in strolling through a nature preserve as compared with a comparable walk in a city setting, including lower blood pressure and better mood (see Hartig, Mitchell, De Vries, & Frumkin, 2014).

Not surprisingly, Dr. Hartig's professional interest in this topic originates in his uplifting early experiences around nature. "I spent much time in the woods behind our home in Michigan while growing up," Hartig (personal communication, March 15, 2015) reminisced, "and I remember those woods fondly as a pleasant place for solitude, as well as a place to retreat with friends. . . . Later, my first hiking trip in the Sierra Nevada of California also provided inspiration and helped me appreciate more of my own capability to persist with difficult challenges."

There is also evidence that nature is not only restorative for us emotionally but beneficial cognitively too. It is interesting to note that it may not actually be necessary to immerse in nature to gain this advantage. For example, an influential study led by Dr. Marc Berman (Berman, Jonides, & Kaplan, 2008) found that college students exposed to nature photos recovered more quickly from a computer task than those shown urban scenes or geometric patterns. In a follow-up experiment in the same study, college students who were exposed to nature photos did better on an attentional task than peers presented with urban photos. Such studies have given rise to attention restoration theory, emphasizing the cognitive payoff for nature experiences.

In this activity, visit a nature site and stroll for a couple of hours. Bring a pen or pencil and sketch pad and draw several scenes that you find appealing. Don't worry, this is not a test of your artistic ability! Please do not bring your laptop or smartphone for this purpose, for these devices tend to be distracting. Focus on the natural world rather than on artificial structures like fences or playgrounds. This activity is not about artistic prowess but rather on heightening your sensitivity to natural beauty. You may not be able to get to a wilderness preserve, but within proximity to nearly every city and town are restorative settings, such as botanical gardens and large parks.

Your Work: **Please use this space, and additional journal space as appropriate, for your work.**

_____

_____

_____

_____

_____

_____

_____

_____

_____

_____

_____

_____

_____

_____

_____

32 AESTHETICS: ART APPRECIATION

For centuries, art galleries and museums have delighted people throughout the world. Such 19th-century literary giants as Edgar Allen Poe and Tolstoy extolled the value of aesthetic experience for human fulfillment, as later psychological theorists including Abraham Maslow and Rollo May did too; but empirical support for this belief remained sparse. Perhaps this research dearth reflected the fact that people vary so much in their overall sensitivity to art—as well in their specific preferences.

However, this situation is now changing. In a study by Daniel Fujiwara (2013) at the London School of Economics, over 14,000 British adults were surveyed on their involvement in cultural and sporting activities. After controlling for many factors, he found that visiting museums enhanced both happiness and self-reported health. Indeed, his participants prized this activity more than playing a sport, doing artwork, or attending sporting events or concerts.

How does museum-going benefit mind and body? An answer may lie in attention restoration theory, developed by Drs. Rachel Kaplan and Stephen Kaplan at the University of Michigan during the 1980s. They were initially interested in how natural settings help people overcome mental fatigue, irritability, and stress. In their view, such activities as hiking through nature elicit several payoffs: *fascination* or engaging our attention in an effortless way; *being away*, or removing ourselves from daily routines; *extent*, or experiencing a venue with sufficient structure and scope to occupy our mind for hours or longer; and *compatibility*, or being in a place that well fits our interests and goals.

As later investigators have argued, art museums often offer these same uplifting qualities—and research led by Dr. Semir Zeki, a neurobiologist at the University College London, suggests that viewing beautiful art evokes the same pleasure physiologically as falling in love. That is, the same part of the brain that is activated when we fall for someone romantically is stimulated when we gaze at artistic masterpieces. Specifically, Zeki (2007) found that viewing art triggers a surge of the "feel-good" chemical dopamine into the orbito-frontal cortex of the brain, resulting in feelings of intense pleasure.

In this activity, visit an art museum or gallery and spend at least 20 minutes with each of two works of art you find beautiful or intriguing. These can be paintings, sculptures, or multimedia installations. Then immediately write about what resonated with you—and what feelings were evoked. Finally, why do you think these works moved you strongly: Was it mainly the artistic medium, subject matter, colors and pattern, or something else?

Write your answers below.

Your Work: **Please use this space, and additional journal space as appropriate, for your work.**

_____

_____

_____

33 AESTHETICS: PHOTOGRAPHY

Is photography just a hobby—or something more vital for personal well-being, a way toward self-realization? The concept of "mindful photography" as it is popularly known originated with Minor White, who studied during the 1940s with such luminaries as Alfred Stieglitz, Ansel Adams, and Edward Weston. Later at MIT, after delving into Zen Buddhism, White taught the importance of meditation and mindfulness for effective photography—and as a way of life. "Be still with yourself until the object of your attention affirms your presence," White (1966) advised—and more broadly observed that "innocence of eye has a quality of its own. It means to see as a child sees, with freshness and acknowledgment of . . . wonder."

Though empirical research remains scant, health professionals are increasingly using photography for its emotional benefits. In 2008, the First International Conference on Phototherapy and Therapeutic Photography took place in Norway. Originally an offshoot of art therapy, the wider use of photography to enhance well-being is gaining popularity through adult classes and workshops. Such programs emphasize how photos can serve as a visual diary for self-insight, enhance positive memories, foster creativity, and strengthen connections with others.

Mindful photography is also being used in the classroom. For example, in a project designed to teach children the concept of well-being, Drs. Saoirse Gabhainn and Jane Sixsmith (2006) at the National University of Ireland instructed a group of 8- to 12-year-olds to take photos of "things they liked," and a follow-up group organized the photos into categories such as "people I love the most," "food and drink," and "animals/pets." This activity proved an effective instructional tool for catalyzing discussion about well-being. A study led by Dr. Yu Chen (Chen, Mark, & Ali, 2014) at the University of California at Irvine used photography to bolster positive functioning among college students. Participants were randomly assigned to one of three experimental conditions: taking a daily selfie with a smiling expression, taking a daily photo of something to make oneself happy, or taking a daily photo of something to make another person happy. In all three conditions, participants increased their positive affect. However, those assigned to make themselves happy became more reflective and those assigned to make another person happy became closer with friends and family members.

This activity involves an adaptation of the above study. Every day for the next week, use your smartphone camera to send a photo to two different family members or friends. The theme can be nature, architecture, or people. Choose one theme for the week and stick with it. Afterward, describe how both you and your recipients were affected by this activity. If you particularly enjoyed it, you may select another theme for a second week and also choose different recipients.

Write about your experience below.

Your Work: **Please use this space, and additional journal space as appropriate, for your work.**

I enjoyed this activity throughout. I have always enjoyed nature and trying to capture the most authentic photos of it. What I appreciated about doing this everyday for a week was I felt more connected to my surroundings that I see everyday and normally don't think much of. To stop and look around for the best possible photo allowed me to further appreciate what I was seeing. There is so much beautiful nature everywhere and we often take it for granted because we're used to seeing it all the time. I feel like trees give me a sense of calm, so I love being surrounded by them. Not only did this activity teach me to appreciate my surroundings, it also helped me capture how my surroundings made me feel in a particular moment. For me, photos always tell stories and are the perfect way to reflect on past experiences, feelings, and emotions. The photos I took this week will always help to remind me to appreciate the constant beauty of nature around me. Plus it was really cool to share my experience of this activity with my family.

34 PASSION

Dr. Robert Vallerand is a Canadian psychologist who has spent his career studying passion. For Vallerand and his colleagues, passion is a strong desire to pursue a self-defining activity that one likes or loves, is highly important to the person, and represents a central feature of the person's identity. Passion is the result of an intense interest and commitment to an activity, to an idea, or to a cause that is central to the person's self-identity. Research has found that 84% of college students reported an activity that they were at least moderately passionate about. Vallerand (2015) also found that not all passion is conducive to optimal well-being.

In their studies of passion, Vallerand and his colleagues postulated a dual model in which two types of passion could be observed. The first is *harmonious* passion, in which autonomous motivation was freely chosen, the activity appeared to "fit" with the person's personality, and the activity was engaged in effortlessly and joyfully. People often reported being in flow or "in the zone" when they engaged in their harmonious passion. Although money or fame might come as a result of their passion, those external rewards are not the primary driver of their involvement.

The second type of passion is *obsessive* passion. This type involves feelings of being controlled; it often involves a rigid persistence in an activity and may create internal self-identity conflicts and even anxiety or shame. Examples are gambling and other addictive behaviors, including Internet addictions. It must be admitted that the dividing line between harmonious and obsessive passion can sometimes be a bit blurry. For example, many people pursue a career in the arts, such as music, because of the harmonious passion they feel for their mode of artistic expression. At the same time, many of those people would also love to make a living with their passion, and the drive for financial security and fame may threaten to turn a harmonious passion into a search for only external rewards.

For the exercise, please think of something you consider a passion. For the next week be sure that you take 10 to 15 minutes every day to engage in your passion in some way (of course, we are talking about a harmonious passion). You may not be able to actually do the activity, but you can read more about it, practice aspects of the activity, or discuss it with people who are also passionate about the activity. If you can't think of something you are passionate about, that's fine. You will find a passion one day. For now, take time every day to learn about anything you are curious about. After all, curiosity often leads to passion. Please write about your experiences in your journal.

Your Work: **Please use this space, and additional journal space as appropriate, for your work.**

_____

_____

_____

35 AESTHETIC APPRECIATION WEEK

For this activity, we would like you to increase your awareness of art and beauty in your world. It is clear to even the most casual observer that the appreciation of beauty is important to people. Cave paintings that are over 30,000 years old display well-developed skill and a keen eye for aesthetics. Tombs and burials that are many thousands of years old contain paintings, spectacular coffins, jewelry, and other objects that leave no doubt the culture valued beauty and took the time to support the artisans who created these objects. Today our lives are filled with objects and artistic expressions created to bring more joy and meaning to life (Martinez-Marti, Hernández-Lloreda, & Avia, 2015).

For the next week, please pay attention to colors, textures, sounds, movement, or even tastes that you encounter. Pay attention to these elements in your experience throughout your day—as you walk or drive, in your home, on campus, as seen on other people, everywhere you go. Note, in this activity you don't need to look for "artistic" expressions. Just notice the world around you on a day-to-day basis. You may also notice everyday elements of your world and recognize that someone had to design every manufactured item in your world. That is, someone had to imagine how everything would look—clothes, buildings, cars, books, iPads, computers, and so on. Someone had to create how each element of your environment would look.

Strive to notice the natural environment as well. The obvious choices are sunrises and sunsets, but look around at the way landscape designers and gardeners have created natural worlds of beauty with shapes, textures, and colors. Try to notice the sounds in your life as well. Listen to the background music in television shows, movies, commercials, videos, and anywhere else where music is part of your experiences. Be aware that beauty can take many forms including aesthetic beauty, natural beauty, and moral beauty. Moral beauty is the experience you get when someone's behavior or a singular experience seems to express the highest virtues and moral potentials of humanity.

Have fun with this exercise, but we would ask you to make sure you try to see something new and look at your world in a way you normally don't. That is, please don't simply repeat activities that you already do or go see art exhibits that you've seen before. Reach out and try something new.

While doing this activity, take time every day to do a little journaling or just take some notes. At the end of a week, review what you wrote and write a brief description of how the activity affected your well-being. It may be helpful to share your feelings or experiences with friends or family members, and remember that even seemingly small events can be recorded as well.

Your Work: **Please use this space, and additional journal space as appropriate, for your work.**

———————————————————————————————————

———————————————————————————————————

8 WELL-BEING ACROSS THE LIFE SPAN

36 RESILIENCE

Everyone will encounter difficult events in life. At times we all need to adapt and adjust to events that are unexpected or unwanted or pose a serious threat to our current and future well-being. Resilience is the ability to recover successfully from these unwanted events and to regain a sense of security, happiness, and hope for the future. Resilience means "bouncing back" from difficult situations. It is important to know that *resilience* is a term usually applied to very difficult situations rather than to daily hassles. That is, bouncing back from an unexpected and painful divorce involves resilience, whereas bouncing back from an unexpected flat tire on the way to work is coping with a daily hassle. Although the unexpected and unwished for events of life are stressful, some developmental psychologists believe that we need to adapt to difficulties in order to develop into more mature and resilient people. In other words, a life without challenges can result in shallowness and missed opportunities for personal growth.

There is evidence that resilience is related to how people construct the "stories" of their lives. That is, resilience is related to how we create our own internal narratives about who we are, what we have dealt with, what we learned, and where we go next in life (McLean, Pasupathi, & Pals, 2007). For this activity, think about a time (or times) in your life that you had to adapt in the face of adversity, tragedy, threats, or major sources of stress: when you faced a quite difficult situation. You knew that if you didn't handle it well, you could slide into bitterness, chronic remorse, a dramatic loss of self-confidence, and even depression.

Once you have an example, please write about how you managed to deal with the situation. If it helps, think about the following questions:

1. What personal resources did I draw on throughout the experience?

2. Was it more helpful for me to change my thinking, my behavior, or both?

3. What did I do to change my emotions toward more hopefulness and/or courage?

4. What event(s) finally turned things around for me so that I began to move forward?

5. Did I find it helpful to rely on people for support, such as friends and family members? If so, which ones?

6. Was it beneficial for me to help someone else at those times? Did it aid to think of someone besides myself?

7. What did I learn about myself during the experience?

8. What kinds of events have been difficult and stressful for me?

9. How have those events typically affected me?

In your journal, please write a self-reflection piece on your answers to these questions. Try to summarize the important aspects of resilience in your life. Note that not everyone is resilient in the same way. Your resilience is unique, so try to express and document your own style of resilience.

Your Work: **Please use this space, and additional journal space as appropriate, for your work.**

_____

_____

_____

_____

_____

_____

_____

_____

_____

_____

_____

_____

_____

_____

37 FLOURISHING IN ADOLESCENCE

In many ways, adolescence is an invention of the modern industrial world—the life span stage in which we establish our personal identity. Generally this means to gain a realistic sense of our strengths and flaws, to develop satisfying mutual relationships with people outside our family, and to choose a financially stable and personally meaningful career. Especially in a highly individualist nation like the United States, this task is often challenging and stressful. With the onset of puberty, the comfort of childhood sharply begins disappearing—yet the autonomy of adult living can seem almost hopelessly far off. It is no wonder that many types of emotional disturbance—such as eating disorders, depression, substance abuse, and self-injurious cutting—are at their peak during this developmental stage.

Hollywood movies, of course, reinforce the stereotype of the angst-ridden American adolescent male or female. Beginning in the post–World War II era, emotionally laden dramas like *Rebel Without a Cause* were eventually followed by absurd comedies like *Ferris Bueller's Day Off* and *Clueless*, then by more wistful films like *Napoleon Dynamite* and *Juno*—all capitalizing on the notion that the teenage years are inevitably filled with despair and rage. In recent years, though, psychological research has shown that many adolescents are coping quite well with stress—and identified the specific individual and social factors that promote resilience.

For example, studies consistently indicate that adolescents are most likely to flourish if they possess high self-esteem and self-compassion, effective strategies for dealing with stress, and the ability to regulate their moods successfully. Also vital for flourishing is strong social support—involving the triad of friendships, good relations with parents, and a sense of belongingness in the peer group. Adolescents with adequate resilience generally have one or more talents, good problem-solving skills, and self-confidence in their ability to handle challenges—the latter characteristic termed self-efficacy by Albert Bandura.

In this activity, interview two teenagers who appear to be flourishing at their age, that is, doing well academically, having friends, and actively involved with a positive hobby or interest, which may include volunteerism. For each one, your questions may include these: What things do you enjoy the most in school? Do you have any hobbies or special interests? Have you decided yet on a possible career? What ways of dealing with stress are most effective for you? Comparing yourself to teenagers who are coping badly with stress, what personal qualities do you have that help you to be more resilient? Finally, what are some aspects in your home life that strengthen your resilience?

Record below the results of your interviews.

Your Work: **Please use this space, and additional journal space as appropriate, for your work.**

_____

_____

38 MINDFUL PARENTING

How often are you mindful—that is, fully present in the moment? This mental quality is increasingly linked to well-being, and for this reason, psychologists have been extending the concept of mindfulness to family life. In a seminal paper, Dr. Larissa Duncan (Duncan, Coatsworth, & Greenberg, 2009) at the University of California in San Francisco originated the model of "mindful parenting," which she linked to listening to one's children with full attention, cultivating emotional awareness and self-regulation in parenting (such as setting an example for calm behavior), and treating one's children with affection and compassion.

The notion that mindful parenting promotes healthy child development is certainly appealing, but is it actually true? Recent research clearly indicates so. For example, a study led by Dr. Caitlin Turpyn (Turpyn & Chaplin, 2016) at George Mason University surveyed parents on their degree of mindful parenting and then analyzed how they conversed with their 12- to 14-year-olds about a conflict in their relationship. The researchers found that parents higher in mindful parenting expressed less negative emotion (such as anger) and shared more positive emotion (such as laughter) compared with those lower in mindful parenting. Additionally, the sharing of positive emotion was associated with less substance abuse among their offspring.

In another study, a research team led by Dr. Justin Parent (Parent, McKee, Mahon, & Foreh, 2016) at the University of Vermont assessed parents' overall mindfulness as well as parental mindfulness and then analyzed their children's extent of emotional problems; the children's ages comprised three groupings: young childhood, middle childhood, and adolescence. For all three groups, higher levels of parental mindfulness—but not overall mindfulness—were associated significantly with better outcomes for children. The implication seems to be that being mindful and being a mindful parent may be two different things. How so? Perhaps because mindfulness training may make you generally more mindful and calm but not necessarily help you cope with a severely tantrumming 6-year-old or a teenager who comes home at 2:00 a.m.—for those types of situations, mindful parenting may be specifically needed.

In this activity, interview two parents—one in each household—who have one or more children younger than 10 years old. Your interview can include these questions: Do you find that you're more mindful with your child(ren) at certain times of the day than others? How about weekends compared to weekdays? If so, are you able to take this fact into account during parenting endeavors throughout the week? When is mindful parenting easiest for you? When is it most difficult? What advice about mindful parenting would you give to a couple who are expecting their first child in a few weeks?

Record below the results of your interviews.

Your Work: **Please use this space, and additional journal space as appropriate, for your work.**

The first parent that I interviewed was my aunt, She has a nine year old son, his name is Alexander. She told me she is more mindful with her child during afternoons, evenings and weekends. She said she would take this into account in parent endeavors during the week. She said being more mindful is easier to do when less is going on at work and her son is being reasonable. She has difficulty when she is overwhelmed with other things and her son is acting up. Her advice to an expecting couple is to take time to just breath, time for just the couple, and time for just yourself. This will help create a balanced life. The second person I interviewed is my neighbor, he has 3 children under 10. He also said he is more mindful on evenings and weekends. It's easy for him to be mindful when his kids are getting along and doing well in school. It's difficult when his kids don't listen or pickup bad habits from their friends down the street. His advice to an expecting couple is to make sure you're always there for your child and project the energy you want to recieve back from them. This will help you build a more positive relationship with your child.

39 MENTORING

Have you ever had a mentor? If so, how has this relationship affected you? In psychological terms, mentoring is based on psychoanalyst Erik Erikson's (1950) concept of *generativity*, which he advanced in his landmark book, *Childhood and Society*. Erikson delineated eight stages of human development from infancy through old age; each presented a specific task or challenge for growth. He associated midlife—the long seventh stage—with that of generativity: care and guidance of subsequent generations. Erikson viewed parenting as the main arena of generativity for most adults. Yet he cogently argued that not all parents devote their generative energies to their own children and that generativity is certainly possible without parenthood. In short, the key issue is supportive involvement with younger persons for societal benefit.

Psychological research has amplified Erikson's work by identifying four types of generativity. These comprise the *biological*, involving begetting, bearing, and nursing one's infant; the *parental*, concerned with child discipline and the transmission of family traditions; the *technical*, consumed with teaching practical skills; and the *cultural*, focusing on transmitting values, such as autonomy or religiosity, prized by the particular culture. More recently, studies have examined why middle-aged people differ from one another in their degree of generativity. For whereas some men and women eagerly nurture younger persons—whether informally or organizationally—others are indifferent or even hostile to mentoring.

What accounts for such striking differences? Much depends on our role models as we grow to adulthood. If we are fortunate enough to have socially involved parents, as well as inspiring teachers and mentors, then we are more likely to cultivate generativity in our own lives. People with high generativity are more involved than others in civic, political, and religious activities. As parents, they are also more likely to emphasize the importance of imparting values and wisdom as part of their child-rearing responsibility. In addition, they are happier than their contemporaries.

In this activity, interview two people: someone who is currently a mentor and someone who is currently a mentee. They can be part of the same dyad, but if so, be sure to interview each one separately. Some relevant questions might include these: Why did you choose to enter into this social relationship? That is, what was your primary motivation? What expectations or goals did you have at the outset of this relationship? To what extent have these been fulfilled? What has been your greatest satisfaction in this relationship? If a large age difference exists between the two of you, is it a challenge in any way? If so, how? Finally, what advice would you give to someone who is contemplating entering into this type of relationship?

Record below the answers you received.

Your Work: **Please use this space, and additional journal space as appropriate, for your work.**

_____

_____

40 FLOURISHING IN OLD AGE

Popular stereotypes—often magnified by Hollywood movies and TV shows—depict older people as fussy, stubborn, and cantankerous. For example, the animated Disney film *Up!* portrays a childless widower constantly snarling at a kindly neighborhood Boy Scout until they eventually become good friends after a harrowing, far-off adventure together. Although the elder protagonist had a toy balloon business before retiring, he had lost nearly all sense of playfulness.

Because most studies on aging until recently have focused almost exclusively on negative aspects including disease, chronic pain, cognitive impairment, and loneliness, playfulness has received meager attention. Fortunately, however, this situation is rapidly changing. In a review of the scientific literature, a team of Israeli researchers stated that "healthy aging is reflected in well-being, participation, playfulness, and cognitive-emotional functioning." In highlighting the importance of playfulness in aging well, they drew substantially upon Dr. René Proyer's work at the University of Zurich. In a variety of studies, Proyer (2013, 2017) has found that playfulness is positively linked with happiness, agreeableness, and physical well-being—quite an appealing combination.

In an important study led by Dr. Po-Ju Chang (Chang & Yarnal, 2018) at National Chung Hsing University, the playfulness of women age 50 and older was found to be a significant factor in strengthening resilience over a year's time. In addition, those women who scored high on playfulness showed greater resilience than their less playful peers. Dr. Chang's research team therefore recommended that programs planned for older adults be designed to increase their playfulness—to improve well-being and health, as well as resilience for later life challenges.

Several measures have been developed to measure adult playfulness, including most recently the Adult Trait Playfulness Scale (ATPS). It comprises such items as "I think that fun is a very important part of life," "I appreciate fun things started by others," "I like to play in my mind," and "I try to have fun no matter what I am doing."

In this activity, interview a man and woman who are both at least 75 years old and living in their own home—either with other people or alone. Your questions may include these: From your experience, is playfulness important for people's health as they get older? How does playfulness make a difference in the lives of older persons? What activities, such as sports, hobbies, and interests, give you a sense of playfulness? Finally, what advice would you give to young adults as to how to incorporate more playfulness in their daily life?

Record below the results of your interviews.

Your Work: **Please use this space, and additional journal space as appropriate, for your work.**

_____

_____

_____

_____

_____

_____

_____

_____

_____

_____

_____

_____

_____

_____

_____

_____

_____

_____

_____

_____

_____

_____

9 MODELS OF OPTIMAL WELL-BEING

41 YOUR BEST POSSIBLE SELF

One of the basic assumptions of positive psychology is that human beings have the potential to conduct themselves with extraordinary competence, compassion, and dignity. Many research areas of positive psychology have focused on what human beings are like when they are operating from their highest potentials.

When researchers examine what people are like when operating from their highest potentials, they are taking a eudaimonic perspective on well-being. As you may recall, eudaimonia focuses on personal growth, optimal personality development, and a search for meaning. With eudaimonia, the primary goals in life involve a search for personal growth and meaning, and happiness and positive emotionality are regarded as by-products of that search.

In this activity, imagine what you will be like when you have realized your best possible self, when you are functioning out of your highest self. We ask you to take the perspective of eudaimonia and think of your best future self in terms of goal attainment, personal growth, and optimal personality development. Therefore, we are not asking you to imagine how much positive emotionality you will feel if you win the lottery at some point in the future. Instead, what will your life be like when you are operating out of your highest potentials?

For the activity, begin by imagining what your life will be like in the future when everything has gone right for you, when everything has gone as well as it possibly could. In this possible future, you have worked hard and achieved your most cherished goals and dreams. In addition, you have developed your positive personality characteristics so that you are living a life in which your motives and intentions are a product of your highest potentials and your daily decisions flow from your best possible self. In your journal, please write about what you will be like in this imagined future. Go into as much detail as you can about what you will have accomplished and what you will be like as a person. Throughout the next week, continue to think about what this imagined future will be like for you.

In addition, use your image of this future to guide your decisions today to enable you to reach this future. This aspect is very important. When you need to make decisions during the next week, whether they are small ones or major, use the image of your best possible future self to guide you. Make choices today that will lead toward that future you want for yourself.

Be sure to monitor how this activity impacted your well-being and if you noticed changes in how you made decisions.

This activity was adapted from Sheldon and Lyubomirsky (2006).

Your Work: **Please use this space, and additional journal space as appropriate, for your work.**

In my future, When I'm operating at my prime, I want to have a job that feels satisfying and pays well enough so that I can live the lifestyle I've always wanted to. In my career I am respected and known as a true professional. I'm not sure yet what exactly that career will be but I'm sure I'll know when the time is right. I will have a loving husband, most likely 2-3 dogs, and potentially young children. I'll have a home that feels comfortable and go all out with decorating it for Christmas. Finally, I'll be able to afford nice vacations throughout the year for my family, my spouse and I, or just me. keeping this vision of my future in mind throughout the week definitely affected my mood and the decisions I made. I felt more confident and motivated towards school during the week because I have in my mind What the result of all my hard work will be. On monday I made the conscious decision to not go out again for Halloween even though all my friends were because I had a math test the next day I hadn't studied at all for. I put my future first and studied all night and after taking the test feel very good about my decision.

42 MEDITATION FOR PERSONAL AND SPIRITUAL GROWTH

For this activity, we would like you to try entering a different state of consciousness, known as meditation. Research on meditation has found that it can enhance many of the personality qualities associated with optimal personality development, such as authenticity, wisdom, self-actualization, and self-transcendence. In fact, such leading personality theorists as Erich Fromm specifically recommend meditation as a practice that can foster positive personality development. Our meditation instructions are presented below. Please try to meditate for 20 minutes a day at least five times during the next week.

Good luck!!

Meditation can be roughly classified into two types: concentration and insight. We will use mindfulness meditation as an example of insight meditation. In the *concentration* type, you choose an object to be the focus of attention (for example, a candle, a symbol, a question, your breath, a word) and you try to maintain a constant focus of attention on that object. The object of attention and your attention to that object remain constant. In *mindfulness* meditation, you focus your attention on the moment-to-moment experiences that appear and disappear in consciousness. Your attention remains constant, but the focus of your attention changes with the flow of your immediate experiences.

To begin meditating, find a place that is relatively free of distractions for the next 20 minutes. Sit in a chair or on a cushion and straighten your back (if you slouch, it's hard to breathe properly). Next, place your hands on your knees, focus your vision about 2 or 3 feet in front of you, and close your eyes about halfway (some people close their eyes completely). Now, focus your attention on your breath for a minute or two to center yourself. You don't have to regulate it, just observe it.

With a *concentration* form of meditation, beginning meditators are usually asked to count their breaths from 1 to 10 and then back to 1 again. If you lose count, just recognize that fact and return to counting from 1 to 10. After about 2 or 3 minutes, concentrate on the object of your meditation (for example, a candle, an image, a word, or continue focusing your attention on your breath). Each time your thoughts distract you, just *gently* return to your focus of concentration. Meditation is not a contest. Be accepting of inevitable distractions as they arise and be persistent in your efforts at attention.

If you would like, you can engage in what is known as "centering prayer." The instructions that Father Thomas Keating gives for centering prayer are virtually identical to the instructions you have for meditation. The main difference is that Father Keating makes more references to "finding God within the silence." If you try centering prayer, then follow the instructions for the concentration form of meditation and with each breath repeat to yourself a word like *peace*, *love*, or *God*.

If you are doing *mindfulness*, keep your attention on your breath, but you do not need to count. Each time you are distracted from your focus on the breath, just silently label the distraction (for example, "thinking," "pain in back," "bored") and allow the experience to fade as you gently place your attention back on your breath, then on the changing experiences of the moment. The real trick at this point is to focus and also remain open to the thoughts and feelings that will inevitably pass through your awareness. You need to find the right balance between focusing your attention and allowing experiences to flow through your awareness. Be aware that mindfulness meditation can be more difficult than it seems. The difficulties, however, do not necessarily mean that you are doing it wrong. Just be aware of distracting thoughts, shifting emotions, and other sensations, and return your attention to the experiences of the moment.

In your journal, please write about what happened. Did you learn something? Did you expand your potentials, even if only in a small way? Small is perfectly all right. Not everyone enjoys this activity, and that's also okay. Just write about what occurred and comment on your experience.

Your Work: **Please use this space, and additional journal space as appropriate, for your work.**

_____

_____

_____

_____

_____

_____

_____

_____

_____

_____

_____

_____

_____

43 RANDOM ACTS OF KINDNESS

Theories of personal growth and optimal personality development are often misunderstood, even by professional psychologists. One of the more persistent myths about theories of personal growth is that they focus exclusively on development of the individual autonomous "self" and are less concerned with interpersonal relationships or the social world. However, a careful reading of the literature on personal growth quickly reveals that all the significant theorists of personal growth are quite concerned with how we interact with other people and how we conduct ourselves in the social world. In fact, concepts such as Adler's social interest, Maslow's self-actualization, Fromm's productive personality, Frankl's self-transcendent person, as well as research on wisdom and authenticity, all explicitly state that healthy personal growth should result in greater concern for other people and higher motivation to be of service to others. All such theorists assert that greater emotional and intellectual maturity should lead people to focus less on their own welfare and more on the needs of others.

For this activity, please practice random acts of kindness (Lyubormirsky, Tkach, & Sheldon, 2004). In a nutshell, this means that you will increase the number of nice or helpful things you do for other people. You don't have to do big "important" acts for people (we are not asking you to donate a kidney to anyone!), but it is important that you do something that allows you to think about other people's daily struggles and allows you to express compassion, caring, or understanding for the challenges we all face every day. Again, your efforts don't have to be "big." You can do little acts that help out someone else. You can hold open a door, volunteer to carry packages, let someone in line when you're in traffic, cook dinner for someone, walk your friend's dog, or pay for a stranger's coffee.

Over the next week, please try to complete at least five random acts of kindness. You can do them all in one day, one per day, or whatever combination you wish. To keep tabs on your experiences, it can help to take time every day to do a little journaling. Jot down your experiences. At the end of the week, review what you wrote and write a brief description of how the activity affected your well-being. Here are a few ideas to make the activity more meaningful: (1) reread your journal entries every few days, (2) share your feelings with friends or family members, and (3) remember that even seemingly small events can be important.

Your Work: **Please use this space, and additional journal space as appropriate, for your work.**

_____

_____

_____

_____

_____

44 | SELF-ACTUALIZATION

For this activity, we would like you to work with Maslow's theory of self-actualization and his ideas on how people can be more self-actualizing. Please note the use of the verb form (that is, "self-actuali*zing*") to indicate that self-actualization is a process that evolves over time. It is not a static state that a person achieves, and when achieved, then the person is "finished" in his or her growth. Most of Maslow's writings on self-actualization are concerned with descriptions of the personality traits and behaviors of people whom he regarded as highly self-actualizing. Maslow spent considerably less time describing how he believed people came to be that way. That is, he devoted little attention to writing about how to be more self-actualizing in a very practical sense.

When Maslow described the process of becoming more self-actualizing, his recommendations would be quite familiar today to a contemporary positive psychologist. For instance, if we put Maslow's recommendations in terms used in positive psychology then he suggested that people focus on their strengths, live by their highest values and virtues, be more mindful, savor more moments, be more authentic, and foster flow experiences. Maslow also had suggestions for how people should cope with the challenges of daily life.

Maslow said that one of the biggest factors that drives us toward greater self-actualization is the challenge we face between security and growth. In other words, when we have to make a choice in our lives, do we remain with what we know and understand (that is, security) or do we try something new, take a risk, and push our limits (that is, growth). He asserted that self-actualizing people choose growth-producing risks over security more often than other people. Note that Maslow didn't claim that they make the growth choice *all the time*, just more often than most people.

For this activity, please think about one or two growth-producing risks that you could take during the next week. That is, try something new that you have been reluctant to do, something that is holding you back from being who you would like to be. *Be careful with this!* Please choose something that you can learn from even if it doesn't work, and if it doesn't work, you won't be emotionally devastated (we don't want anyone needing to see a therapist because of this activity!). And remember that Maslow never stated that highly self-actualizing people always succeed with the growth-producing risks they take. What he did say was that such individuals learn from what happened; they could grow and develop no matter what occurred.

In your journal, please describe what happened with this activity. What did you learn? Did you enhance your capabilities in any way? Remember that if you choose growth and you fail in your initial effort, that experience can still be growth-producing.

Your Work: **Please use this space, and additional journal space as appropriate, for your work.**

_____

_____

_____

_____

_____

_____

_____

_____

_____

_____

_____

_____

_____

_____

_____

_____

_____

_____

_____

_____

_____

_____

_____

45   YOUR PERSONAL HEROES

When people evaluate their lives in terms of satisfaction or happiness, they often compare themselves to others. In doing so, we can compare ourselves with those who we think are doing better than we are (upward social comparisons), those who are in the same situation we are (lateral social comparisons), or those who are less fortunate than we are (downward social comparisons). People who report being frequently happy use all of these comparisons in very strategic ways to enhance their well-being. For example, they use upward social comparison in recognizing the personality traits, talents, or skills of other people and admiring those people as a way to self-motivate and emulate. In other words, the admiration is used to try becoming a better person rather than belittling one's own abilities.

We all need heroes in our lives. We all need people we can look up to and admire, people we can try to be like, and people we can emulate as role models. Our heroes can be groups of people who do specific jobs, such as firefighters, or groups of people who try to accomplish certain goals, such as Olympic athletes. Often the best heroes are specific people we admire. These can be individuals for whom we have a deep respect and admiration. They may be our favorite musicians, writers, athletes, scientists, or religious figures. Of course, our heroes may also be people whom we know personally.

For this activity, write down the names of people you admire or consider your heroes. List what you like about them: that is, what qualities do they have that you admire? Here's the important part. Do not simply idealize or idolize the people on your list. No one knows what life is really like for other people, so don't project your own fantasies of "perfection" onto your heroes. Rather, write about how they inspire you to be better, how they serve as role models for your life, and how you can learn from them and integrate their admirable qualities into your life. For one week, take an opportunity each day to actualize a quality you admire in your heroes. For instance, if you admire the truthfulness in one of your heroes, then find a way to apply more honesty to a situation in your life.

You may also wish to visit a website created by Dr. Phillip Zimbardo on the Heroic Imagination Project (https://www.heroicimagination.org). Dr. Zimbardo stated that the heroes project is dedicated to "developing and spreading the conception of heroes as ordinary, everyday people who are motivated to act on behalf of others or for a moral cause with action that is extraordinary." We all can be heroes who exhibit moral courage in challenging situations. The world will surely be a better place as more people learn to access their own inner hero.

Your Work: **Please use this space, and additional journal space as appropriate, for your work.**

_____

_____

_____

_____

_____

_____

_____

_____

_____

_____

_____

_____

_____

_____

_____

_____

_____

_____

_____

_____

10 RELIGION, SPIRITUALITY, AND WELL-BEING

46 | THE GRATITUDE EXERCISE

For this activity, we would like you to think about someone who has done you a great service. Think of someone to whom you owe a debt of gratitude and yet have never expressed it. Gratitude is often described as one of the sacred emotions. It is given this largesse because being grateful allows us to think of other people and how they have helped us through life. Being grateful allows us to drop the pretense that we are independent and don't need other people. It allows us to be more humble and acknowledge the debts we all owe to the kindness and assistance we receive from others.

The gratitude activity is one of the "classic" exercises in positive psychology. That is, the activity has been used in positive psychology for more than 15 years. In addition, the activity has been the subject of various research studies. In the classic form, the activity involves thinking of someone to whom one owes a debt of gratitude but has never expressed it. This person can be anyone who has touched you in your life. It may be a friend or relative currently active in your life or someone from your past that you haven't seen in years. Next, the activity involves writing a letter to this person and relate how much you appreciate what he or she has done for you. Really express how you feel. Tell how much that support has meant to you and how grateful you are. In the original activity, participants were asked to hand deliver the letter to the person.

However, for this activity, it is not necessary that you deliver it by hand, although you may do that if you wish. Of course, some people find it more meaningful to simply talk with the person directly and verbalize what's in the written letter. Others may prefer to send the letter and not have any direct contact with the recipient.

Please be aware of one caution with this activity. Some recipients of a gratitude letter may feel embarrassed to be on the receiving end of a heartfelt expression of gratitude. Their embarrassment can cause an awkward social situation, even though they may be quite appreciative of your letter. Therefore, be prepared and accepting of whatever reaction you find from the recipient of your letter.

For your journal entry, please write about your experience with this activity. Research on the gratitude activity can be found at Seligman, Steen, Park, and Peterson (2005).

Your Work: Please use this space, and additional journal space as appropriate, for your work.

_____

_____

_____

_____

_____

_____

_____

_____

_____

_____

_____

_____

_____

_____

_____

_____

_____

47 | LOVING-KINDNESS MEDITATION

For this activity, we would like you to try a specific type of meditation called loving-kindness meditation. It is designed to enhance feelings of compassion, empathy, and goodwill for yourself and other people. The specific form of loving-kindness meditation described in this activity comes out of the Tibetan Buddhist meditative tradition, although similar forms can be found in all contemplative spiritual traditions. Research studies have found that this style of loving-kindness meditation can be quite effective in generating positive emotions and feelings of compassion and caring.

As we noted in the earlier meditation activity, meditation can be loosely classified into two types: concentration and insight. Loving-kindness meditation is a concentration type of meditation. Please refer to the instruction on how to practice a concentration style of meditation given in the earlier activity titled Meditation for Personal and Spiritual Growth. Please try loving-kindness meditation for 10 to15 minutes per day at least five times during the next week. The meditation instructions are presented below.

LOVING-KINDNESS MEDITATION

This version of loving-kindness meditation is composed of five sections of approximately equal length. Your aim is to focus wholly on radiating kindness and compassion to yourself and others. This loving-kindness is to be performed altruistically, without any desire for reward and without discrimination. We do not have to feel that we "like" other people in order for us to share loving-kindness with them. All people are in need of loving-kindness, and we can choose to open up to this idea through meditation. Repeat the phrases below slowly and carefully with an open heart and mind. The classic phrases for the first section are these:

May I live in safety.

May I be happy.

May I be healthy.

May I live with ease. (repeat 3 times)

For each subsequent section, simply substitute the name or image of a person for "I." For example, in the second section you focus on a friend. Therefore, if your friend's name is Joseph you would say, "May Joseph live in safety. May Joseph be happy. May Joseph live with ease." Here are the five sections:

- First section—Yourself ("May I live in safety. May I be happy.")

- Second section—A friend

- Third section—A neutral person (someone you see often but do not know well)

- Fourth section—A difficult person (someone whom you have trouble with but not someone you hate)

- Fifth section—"All people" or "all sentient beings"

Therefore, the entire sequence involves 15 repetitions of the classic phrase involving five recipients of your good wishes. Yep, if you do this for 10 minutes, you will be saying the preceding phrase a lot! However, please don't rush through it. Take your time and feel the emotions.

For your journal, please describe what the experience was like for you. If it was pleasant, then why? If not, why? What difficulties, if any, were involved? If this activity was not uplifting for you, that's all right. Just write about what happened and comment on your experience.

See the following studies for relevant research on loving-kindness meditation: Fredrickson, Cohn, Coffey, Pek, and Finkel (2008); Hutcherson, Seppala, and Gross (2008).

Your Work: Please use this space, and additional journal space as appropriate, for your work.

I throughouly enjoyed this activity and believe I got a lot out of it. Most sections were easy and felt natural to say, the two I thought most about were the third and fourth sections. The neutral person was someone I sit next to in math that seems really nice + cool but I've been too anxious to talk to. This activity made me realize its worth a shot to try and get to know them. The hardest was a difficult person because I am currently working on a group project for class and one of the members really annoys me. The activity helped me to acknowledge those feelings and wish the best for him anyway. I have no choice but to work with him and I likely will never see him again after so there's no point in wasting energy basking in my annoyance. I love the practice of wishing the best for everyone and being able to move on if they are not right for your life.

48 FORGIVENESS

Is it easy for you to forgive others, or do you often fixate on experiences when people have hurt or disappointed you? It is hardly coincidental that both Eastern and Western spiritual traditions venerate the sage as one with a forgiving outlook. Drawing on millennia of religious teaching, Dr. Martin Luther King (1967) stated, "We must develop and maintain the capacity to forgive. He who is devoid of the power to forgive is devoid of the power to love."

Learning to forgive is not always easy. Many people get bogged down between their intent and their subsequent behavior. For this reason, Dr. Robert Enright (2001) of the University of Wisconsin at Madison—a leading researcher in this field—has proposed that forgiveness is rather complex and involves four steps: *uncovering* one's emotions of anger or resentment; *deciding* to forgive; *working* to reframe an incident through insight and empathy; and *deepening* one's sense of meaning as a result of one's injury. By following through on these four steps, individuals can lower their worry and distress.

Scientific evidence is mounting about the health benefits of forgiveness. For example, people who have forgiven others for a major transgression have lower blood pressure and heart rates as compared to those who remain unforgiving. One investigation found that sleep quality—which has been found to affect many aspects of our physical health—is affected by thoughts of revenge; people suffering from insomnia were more likely to have bitter thoughts than those whose minds were at peace. Similarly, cardiac patients with forgiving personalities had less depression and anxiety about their condition than did their less forgiving peers.

Psychological research also reveals that as we get older, we tend to become more forgiving. This finding probably reflects the fact that increasing chronological age helps us to see the "big picture" of life in better perspective—a central feature of wisdom. In this sense, the ability to forgive is a trait we all can strengthen in order to gain new opportunities for happiness.

In this activity, interview two people over the age of 40. Your questions may include the following: What actions are easiest for you to forgive in others? Why do you think this is true for you? In contrast, what actions are more difficult for you to forgive and why? In your view, are certain acts unforgivable? Have you ever decided to forgive someone for a misdeed, and if so, how did you feel afterward? If you noticed an effect, was it immediate or gradual?

Write your answers below to these questions.

Your Work: **Please use this space, and additional journal space as appropriate, for your work.**

_____

_____

_____

_____

49 A SENSE OF WONDER

"Imagination is more important than knowledge," stated Albert Einstein (1972), "for imagination embraces the entire world, and all there ever will be to know and understand." In his widely read philosophical essays, Einstein extolled wonder as a key driver for both creativity and scientific discovery—and urged that schools better cultivate this trait.

For many decades, academic psychology had meager interest in this quality. However, the situation began to change with Abraham Maslow's studies of self-actualizing men and women—individuals who maximized their potential in daily life. Maslow found that these highly successful, creative people had frequent peak experiences, whose essence often involved a sense of wonder. He strongly endorsed Einstein's view that education should promote more experiences of wonderment, to help produce creative scientists and artists.

In earlier times, organized religion provided a sense of wonder to ordinary as well as highly talented individuals. Sacred texts like the Bible inspired the imagination of countless generations via tales of angels and prophets, dreamers and kings, apocalyptic battles, and journeys to heaven. It seems no historical accident that precisely when such religious narratives lost much of their popular appeal in the late 19th century, their place was taken by fantasy and science fiction—offering fresh images and ways of experiencing the universe. As literary critic David Hartwell (1996) has commented, "science fiction has claimed the domains of time (especially the distant future) and space, the infinite possibilities out there, just at the moment when the last location of awe and mystery have disappeared from our planet."

It's not surprising, therefore, that Maslow himself—one of America's most creative psychological thinkers—valued sci-fi as a precious source of new ideas about human nature and society. More recently, Dr. Tonie Stolberg (2008) of England's Birmingham University has studied real experiences of wonderment in the life histories of college students planning a career in science education. Exactly as Einstein would have predicted, such experiences were indeed common and impacted their vocational choice.

To strengthen your sense of wonder, it's important to nurture your imagination. An excellent way is to keep a dream diary, for dreams alter our perceptions of time and space: We fly like birds, we see dinosaurs, we travel to far-off planets. Keep a notepad and pencil on your nightstand, and each morning for a week, write down your dream—even if it's only fragmentary. Over time, you'll find that your dream recall steadily improves. If you still have trouble catching a dream, set your smartphone alarm to wake you in the middle of the night, and then immediately write your dream. What strikes you in each dream as most imaginative?

Your Work: **Please use this space, and additional journal space as appropriate, for your work.**

_____

_____

50 MORAL ELATION

Did you know that Thomas Jefferson helped to create a new specialty in positive psychology? Surprisingly, America's third president gave rise to the study of moral elation (sometimes called elevation), that is, our feeling of joy when witnessing an act of goodness. Several years ago, Dr. Jonathan Haidt of New York University was fascinated by Jefferson's (1771) posthumously published letter to a friend stating that "when any original act of charity or gratitude is presented either to our sight or imagination, we are deeply impressed with its beauty—and feel a strong desire in ourselves of doing charitable and grateful acts also."

Dr. Haidt wondered if Jefferson's intriguing comment was scientifically accurate, and a series of psychological experiments confirmed that it was. Both subjectively in terms of the individual's feelings and objectively involving measurable consequences, moral elation proved a distinct emotional state—different from, say, enjoying a delicious meal. In physical terms, moral elation is associated with "feeling moved and uplifted, having a warm feeling in the chest, and wanting to become a better person . . . and to help others" (Haidt, 2000).

Among today's leading researchers of moral elation is Dr. Ryan Niemic of Xavier University. In his view, it can manifest in several possible ways after we see an inspiring movie character or theme. We may decide to imitate the protagonist's core strengths in order to improve ourselves or others; for example, *The Shawshank Redemption* induces some viewers to use more hope and perseverance in their own lives. Others, after watching a movie like *The Artist*, decide to express a strength or virtue different from what was portrayed— such as gratitude for life rather than zest. And still others become motivated to "do good" or improve themselves through a changed outlook. From our professional experience, films often mentioned in this context include *As Good as It Gets*, *Finding Forrester*, *The Truman Show*, and, of course, director Frank Capra's classic *It's a Wonderful Life*.

In this activity, identify four movies you've seen that evoked moral elation for you— such as portraying compassion, courage, resolve, or altruism. These can be documentaries involving biography or history, as well as dramas based on true-life events or those entirely fictional. For each film, describe in a few sentences the specific scene that produced moral elation for you—and whether it involved action, dialogue, or both aspects together. Finally, note whether you suspected beforehand that you'd be powerfully moved or inspired by the movie, or if this effect caught you unawares.

Your Work: **Please use this space, and additional journal space as appropriate, for your work.**

_____

_____

_____

_____

11 POSITIVE INSTITUTIONS AND CULTURAL WELL-BEING

51 CALLINGS

Do you feel that you've found your calling in life—that is, an activity that gives you a sense of overriding meaning, purpose, and constructive contribution to the world? It could be a field of study like education or medicine leading to rigorous work, volunteer efforts that absorb your attention and time, or dedicated caregiving to family members. Before the Industrial Revolution, the notion of "having a calling" was usually associated with religion—especially concerning men and women who felt that God had called them to be clergy. However, vocational researchers today generally agree that people can have a calling without possessing religious belief at all.

In Abraham Maslow's studies of self-actualizing persons, he found that they unfailingly had a sense of mission in life related to their particular skills, talents, and core interests. Indeed, he asserted that not a single self-actualizing individual—at least in Western Europe or the Americas—lacked this characteristic. Though Maslow focused on famous scientists, thinkers, and political leaders who regarded their work as a life mission, he also recognized that family devotion could be a calling. For example, Maslow identified his aunt Pearl as a self-actualizing person whose unstinting, loving care to her large extended family constituted a calling. He would not have been surprised to learn, therefore, that researchers today have begun to identify parenthood as a calling.

For example, a study led by Dr. Justin Coulson (2012) at the University of Wollongong developed a scale to measure parents' subjective sense of calling in child-rearing—containing such items as "Being a parent is central to how I see myself," "I put my children first," and "I can't wait to spend time with my children." The investigators found that parents who regarded child-rearing as their calling had higher parenting pleasure, a lower sense of parenting burden, and greater overall life meaning compared to parents who did not view child-rearing as their calling.

In this activity, interview two people over the age of 35 who view their work or their parenthood as a calling. Your questions may include these: When did you first decide that you had found your calling in life? Was there a specific incident that triggered this awareness—and if so, what was it? Or did you experience a gradual realization? What personal benefits have you experienced in having a calling? Have there also been disadvantages that you can identify? Finally, what advice would you give to a college student who is searching for his or her calling in life?

Record below the results of your interviews.

Your Work: **Please use this space, and additional journal space as appropriate, for your work.**

The first person I interviewed was my dad. He said he found his calling in life through helping others, after he got his masters degree. There wasn't something specific that drew him to this, he's always been passionate about helping others. Its beneficial to him because he feels that he is fulfilling his life purpose. A disadvantage is he sees a lot of people struggling & has to hear their heartbreaking stories, this can be very depressing. His advice to a student is to let things fall into place. His major in college has nothing to do with what he does today. The second interview was with my aunt. Her calling is being a mother and she realized that when she saw her son for the first time. She feels satisfaction in being able to raise a person she created & feels that was her purpose in life. A disadvantage is being a mother can get extremely stressful. Her advice is to only do things that make yourself feel good, having a positive mindset is the most important thing in life.

52 VOLUNTEERING

If you're seeking to boost your well-being, volunteerism is an admirable way to do it. In fields today ranging from secondary education to gerontology, researchers are increasingly confirming the mind–body benefits of volunteerism; the effect begins as early as adolescence and continues all the way through old age.

Concerning the younger end of the chronological spectrum, studies show that teens who volunteer are less likely to become pregnant or use drugs—and are more likely to have positive scholastic, psychological, and vocational functioning than nonvolunteering peers. There's an important health payoff as well. As reported by Dr. Hannah Schreier and her colleagues (Schreier, Schonert-Reichl, & Chen, 2013) at New York's Mount Sinai School of Medicine, 10th graders who participated in a 2-month mentoring program with elementary-school-age children showed lower cholesterol levels and body mass compared to controls; the impact was greatest for teens who became more empathic and altruistic by volunteering.

How about for midlife and beyond? In a study by Drs. Peggy Thoits and Lyndi Hewitt (2001) at Vanderbilt University, volunteering adults scored higher than nonvolunteers on six aspects of personal well-being: happiness, life satisfaction, self-esteem, sense of control over life, physical health, and rarity of depression. The researchers also found evidence for a personality-and-volunteerism cycle—in which people who are happier and have higher self-esteem are more likely to volunteer, thereby further boosting their well-being. More recently, Drs. Martin Binder and Andreas Freytag (2013) reported that volunteerism sustained over time steadily raised individuals' happiness—and, strikingly, no "drop-off effect" in mood occurred. The investigators recommended that public policymakers more strongly encourage adult volunteering—such as by publicizing its payoff in greater personal happiness.

The scientific evidence is compelling too regarding those in retirement years. In a representative study led by Dr. Nancy Morrow-Howell (2003) at Washington University, older adults who volunteer—and who engage in more hours of volunteering—reported higher levels of well-being, regardless of gender or race, compared to nonvolunteers similar in mental and physical health.

In this activity, volunteer for a cause that personally interests you. It may involve improving parks in your area, promoting the arts, or reading to schoolchildren. First identify the skills you can offer and then decide whether you want to learn something new, for many organizations will train volunteers. If you're limited by time or transportation access, it's possible to help by Internet or phone. Also, consider volunteering with a family member or friend; you're likely to become closer by helping others. At the end of your volunteer experience, write a page about how it impacted you emotionally.

Your Work: **Please use this space, and additional journal space as appropriate, for your work.**

_____

_____

53 LEADERSHIP

When it comes to leadership, do you have "the right stuff" (the title of an influential movie about the U.S. space program for training astronauts)? Can you be a leader even if you're not a politician or general, a famous sports coach, or head of a multinational corporation? The study of leadership has become a major arena in organizational psychology and business alike, simply because effective leaders indeed have tremendous impact on their respective enterprise as well as scientific, scholastic, and artistic fields. Many of the psychological studies on creative leadership emphasize these three elements: (1) optimism and excitement about the future, (2) a preference to think in "big picture" terms rather than concentrating on minute details and micromanaging issues, and (3) an outlook that values individuals for their unique talents and seeks to optimize their growth as the building blocks of organizational success.

Since the 1990s, colleges have devoted increasing attention to student leadership development. It has been estimated that more than 1,000 such programs now exist in the United States, with a growing focus on volunteerism, social change, and service to others. Community service experience, particularly involving facets of citizenship and collaboration, has been found prevalent among participants. What does personality research reveal about college student leaders? A study led by Dr. Rose Marie Ward (Ward, DiPaola, & Popson, 2009) found that female student leaders tended to be extroverts with good relations with their parents—especially with their mother—to be eager to identify and perform as a leader, and to have self-perceptions of emotional-physical strength. Research by Dr. Christen Logue and her colleagues (Logue, Hector, & Hutchens, 2005) found that student leaders overwhelming relished their leadership role—especially the aspects of action, motivating others, participating in a team or community endeavor, and giving benevolently to others. More recently, a study by Drs. Edward Hoffman and Catalina Acosta-Orozco (2015) reported that college student leaders expressed life metaphors that were mainly active, individualistic, and affectively positive; they also stated that their life metaphor strongly impacted their motivation and decision-making.

In this activity, interview two students at your college who currently hold or have held a leadership position—such as in campus government, an academic club, or a collegiate community, political, or religious association. Your questions might include these: What motivated you to take this position? Did it already exist, or did you create it? If the latter situation, why did you decide to initiate this position? What have been your greatest satisfactions in the student leadership role? Finally, what skills do you feel are most important in the student leadership role, and why?

Your Work: **Please use this space, and additional journal space as appropriate, for your work.**

_____

_____

54 | WORLDVIEWS AND WHY THEY MATTER

In a sentence, what is your metaphoric view of human existence? Is it a journey (as most people in the West express) or more akin to a roller coaster or a roulette wheel? How about a game of strategy like chess? And what is your metaphor for love relationships: a wonderful duet, an adventure, or a stormy sea? Psychologists increasingly believe that your answers to these questions impact your decision-making and actions in daily life.

Though metaphors for human nature come and go with regularity, it was Alfred Adler who first argued in the 1930s that everyone has a specific metaphor for dealing with life. In Adler's (1930, 1938) view, we develop our life plan quite early, and it is firmly in place by the age of 6. It represents our particular way of managing life's uncertainties and is connected to what psychologists today term our worldview. Where does it originate? For Adlerians, our worldview comes mainly from our inborn strengths and weaknesses (physical as well as mental) and from our early experiences with parents and siblings. Adler stated that our worldview is often revealed by our metaphors—and has important consequences for our daily life. Research today shows that a cynical worldview ("People are basically selfish, so be on guard with them") is associated with lower mental and physical health, whereas a benevolent worldview ("People are basically kindly, so reach out to them") may bring benefits in both realms.

Therapists and life coaches now increasingly focus on the root metaphors that people use to describe their personal lives, careers, and relationships. As George Lakoff and Mark Johnson (1980) declared in their seminal book *Metaphors We Live By*, "metaphors are not mere poetical or rhetorical embellishments. They affect the ways in which we perceive, think, and act. Reality itself is defined by metaphor" (p. 3).

Over the past few years, we have collaborated on research to better understand life metaphors—and how these vary by such aspects as our age, occupation, and nationality. For example, we found that college student leaders expressed life metaphors that were optimistic, active, and individualistic rather than gloomy, passive, or impersonal.

In this activity, take a few minutes and complete this phrase with a sentence: Life is like a(n) _____. Then allow time for some self-analysis. For instance, would you say that your worldview—as expressed by your life metaphor—is optimistic, pessimistic, or somewhere in between? Is it mainly individualistic or more socially oriented? Is it basically active or passive? How long have you had this worldview? Can you identify when it originated? And, if you would like to experience greater daily happiness, what other possible metaphors beckon to you?

Write your answers below.

Your Work: **Please use this space, and additional journal space as appropriate, for your work.**

_____

_____

55 TRAVEL

Do you like to travel? For many people, it's one of life's most fulfilling experiences—not only inducing pleasant relaxation but also offering new philosophical and spiritual vistas. Such founders of modern psychology as Alfred Adler and Carl Jung traveled extensively to promote their work. Both not only reveled in the attention they received from diverse audiences but also gained important insights into how cultures influence personality. Yet, surprisingly, neither ever discussed the psychological benefits of travel.

Fortunately, this situation is now changing. Among the world's leading psychological researchers on travel is Dr. Sebastian Filep (2007) of the University of Otago in New Zealand. In recent years, his studies have highlighted the link between tourist experiences and positive functioning—especially that of *flow*. It may arise, for example, when we are captivated by beautiful scenery or historic architecture—and fall into a dreamy, delightful state of timelessness.

In forging a new approach to tourism, Dr. Filep has identified five types of experience, each with its special value: *recreational*, which provides general well-being and idle pleasure; *diversionary*, which mainly offers distraction from current stress; *experiential* and *experimental*, which involve respectively a search for self-authenticity and alternative ways of living; and *existential*, which may transform our habitual patterns of thinking or acting. Though we are perhaps most likely to gain flow via the fun of *recreational* and *diversionary* tourism, it is probably the *existential* mode that leads most to enduring personal change.

There is also evidence that foreign travel enhances our creativity. In research that has generated substantial interest in the business community, Drs. William Maddux and Adam Galinsky (2009) found that MBA students—both in the United States and Europe—who had lived abroad were significantly more creative on a variety of problem-solving tasks. In the researchers' view, the experience of living abroad enhances receptivity to new meanings for everyday situations. A study led by Dr. Lile Jia (Jia, Hirt, & Karpen, 2009) at the University of Indiana showed that simply placing ourselves in a "traveling mindset" may also improve creative problem-solving.

In this activity, interview two people (preferably a man and a woman) you know who like to travel, whether for business or pleasure. Your questions may include these: What makes travel enjoyable for you? Do you prefer to travel alone, with friends, with family members, or in a large group? Has travel strengthened your open-mindedness concerning other people or your appreciation for nature? If so, how? In what ways do you think that travel enhances your creativity? Finally, where would you most like to travel next, and why?

Record below the results of your interviews.

Your Work: **Please use this space, and additional journal space as appropriate, for your work.**

_____

_____

12

A LOOK TOWARD THE FUTURE OF POSITIVE PSYCHOLOGY

56 NEGATIVE EMOTIONS AND WELL-BEING

The field of positive psychology quite clearly shows favoritism toward positive emotions. The topics covered by researchers in positive psychology all examine emotional states that are at least mildly pleasant and often may be joyous or even spiritually self-transcendent. Although this state of affairs is relatively self-evident and essentially defines positive psychology, virtually all positive psychologists recognize that negative emotions are a necessary part of a life well lived (Kashdan & Biswas-Diener, 2014). No one who is considered a serious researcher in positive psychology suggests that we should all strive toward unrealistic, blissful states that ignore negative feelings and experiences. Nonetheless, unanswered questions remain about how to balance positive and negative emotions and what types of negative emotions are needed to create a full life. This activity is designed to get you thinking about these questions.

To begin, imagine your life in the future and answer the following questions. Please answer in a realistic way, rather than giving some idealized vision of your future. That is, we assume that no one ever feels ecstatically happy 100% of the time.

When I achieve my ideal of well-being, *on average* my emotions over time will be distributed as follows (note that totals must equal 100%):

Percentage of time I will feel happy _____

Percentage of time I will feel unhappy _____

Percentage of time I will feel neutral _____

Total = 100%

When I achieve my ideal of well-being, *on average* the strength or intensity of my positive emotions over time will be distributed as follows:

Very happy (elated) _____

Pretty happy (spirits high) _____

Mildly happy (cheerful) _____

Slightly happy (a bit above neutral) _____

When I achieve my ideal of well-being, *on average* the strength or intensity of my negative emotions over time will be distributed as follows:

Slightly unhappy (a bit below neutral) _____

Mildly unhappy (sad but functioning okay) _____

Pretty unhappy (tired, uninvolved, dispirited) _____

Very unhappy (very sad, mild hopelessness) _____[2]

What do your answers tell you about your own ideals of happiness, satisfaction with life, well-being, and flourishing? How different is your ideal of well-being from your current balance and intensity of well-being? When you thought about the frequency of negative emotions, were there any specific negative emotions you regarded as necessary for a full life? If you did not consider this question, then please do so now. That is, what negative emotions do we need to feel in order to develop emotionally? Is there any way to recognize when negative emotions are too intense or too frequent? Similarly, although this may seem like an odd question, is there any way to recognize when positive emotions are too intense or too frequent?

Your Work: **Please use this space, and additional journal space as appropriate, for your work.**

_____

_____

_____

_____

_____

_____

_____

_____

---

[2] Please note that if your answers indicated you will feel extremely depressed most of the time, then you should seek professional help as soon as you can.

57 THE HAPPINESS PILL

It will be no surprise that positive psychology studies positive emotions, positive behaviors, and positive ways of thinking. One of the founding assumptions of positive psychology was that it would adopt a scientific approach to the study of well-being. Much of the research has evaluated theories or assessment instruments and has tended to be academic. Nonetheless, the ultimate goal of the research has been to help people achieve a greater sense of well-being and flourishing. All the activities presented in this workbook have been practical applications of the research and theories in positive psychology. The assumption is that if we *do something* to change how we behave, how we think, how we interact with others, or how we use our time, then we can increase our level of well-being or flourishing by those efforts. What if there is another way?

For this activity, imagine that the pharmaceutical industry has just released a "happiness pill." Of course, there have been antidepressant medications on the market for many years. But this pill is designed to elevate the mood of "average" people who are functioning fine in day-to-day life but who are just not flourishing. That is, the effects of the happiness pill are similar to the effects one would expect from practical interventions designed to increase well-being and flourishing. By the way, there is every reason to believe that a pill like this will be available in the near future—this is not an effort in science fiction.

Here are a few caveats to consider. First, the pill is not physically addicting. Second, it is not a "mania pill" that produces unrealistic, ecstatic emotions and totally blocks out negative emotions. It simply creates an emotional bias for the positive end of the spectrum. Third, a person will not habituate to the effects so that these will remain effective over the passage of time. Finally, the pill is affordable. Clearly, the next question is this: Will you take the happiness pill?

Here are a few things to think about as you decide on your answer. A few advantages of the happiness pill are that it is easy, effective, and reliable. A disadvantage is that it produces an artificial form of happiness, and by taking the pill, a person loses that sense of personal accomplishment that comes from working hard to achieve a goal: in this case, the goal of increasing personal flourishing. Another disadvantage is that the happiness pill would not be effective when a person encounters difficult life events that are unexpected and unwanted. That is, because the pill induces a sense of well-being without the individual's having undergone struggle and adaptation, one may not have learned the coping skills needed to deal with significant setbacks and challenges.

Please take some time and think about other advantages and disadvantages. In your journal, write about why you would or would not take the happiness pill.

Your Work: **Please use this space, and additional journal space as appropriate, for your work.**

_____

_____

58 THE EAST ASIAN APPROACH TO WELL-BEING

Just as positive psychology has roots in the West that date back millennia, so too for East Asia—encompassing mainland China, Japan, and the Korean peninsula, as well as Taiwan, Hong Kong, Macau, and Mongolia. For people in this region, traditional concepts and values about well-being come from three main sources: Buddhism, Confucianism, and Taoism. For example, Confucius taught that people can achieve happiness in life by satisfaction of basic needs, acting kindly to others, and contributing to society. Buddhism emphasizes the impermanence of human life, acceptance of suffering, and eliminating selfish desires through mindfulness. Taoism relates that happiness can be acquired by appreciating the beauty of nature and truly seeing the unity of all existence.

East Asian cultures today are changing rapidly—all moving in the direction of greater individualism. For instance, China's sweeping economic transformation in the past 25 years has led many young adults to link their happiness and life satisfaction with personal career achievement. In contrast, older Chinese are more likely to still embrace a collectivist outlook and feel pride in national accomplishments. Nevertheless, for both age groups, the traditional cultural values of self-discipline, daily effort, and maximum education attainment remain prominent.

In Japan today, cultural changes are perhaps even more dramatic, driven by relentless demographics. One third of all Japanese people are age 60 or older—and for a country that social scientists not long ago viewed as the pinnacle of collectivism, it is striking to note that a greater percentage of Japanese people now live in one-person households (32.5%) than do Americans (28.1%). Nevertheless, many long-standing cultural values still dominate, such as politeness, orderliness in public, and suppression of emotions. As for South Korea, rapid economic growth and industrialization during the past 20 years have greatly weakened traditional values associated with filial piety and close extended family ties.

In this activity, interview two people who were raised by East Asian immigrants to the United States; your interviewees themselves may have been born in the United States or elsewhere. Your questions may include these: In your view, how do your country's traditional values about the importance of maintaining group harmony differ from the values of mainstream Anglo-American culture? For example, is well-being related more to group belongingness than it is for Anglo-Americans? In your experience, is respect for one's parents, teachers, and the elderly also valued more? How about the definition of success; in your experience, do East Asians define it differently than do their Anglo-American counterparts? If so, how?

Record below the results of your interviews.

Your Work: **Please use this space, and additional journal space as appropriate, for your work.**

_____

_____

_____

_____

_____

_____

_____

_____

_____

_____

_____

_____

_____

_____

_____

_____

_____

_____

_____

_____

_____

_____

_____

59 THE LATINO/A APPROACH TO WELL-BEING

As the United States becomes increasingly diverse demographically, it is crucial for positive psychology to adopt a cross-cultural perspective about individual happiness, meaning, and flourishing. This issue is especially salient today with respect to our country's Latino/a population, which is the largest and most rapidly growing ethnic group. For the purposes of this chapter, *Latino/a* is used instead of *Hispanic* because it is more inclusive of the diversity and ethnic identify of cultural groups whose ancestry is Latin America, Spain, or Spanish-speaking communities.

Unfortunately, the psychology research literature regarding Latino/as residing in the United States has focused predominantly on dysfunction and pathology—such as substance abuse, child maltreatment, juvenile delinquency, gang participation, academic failure, and high school dropout characteristics. Relatively scarce are studies that consider or measure Latino/a strengths and assets—whether at the unit of the individual, family, or community. Such conceptual biases may reflect a genuine desire to ameliorate pressing social problems often linked to poverty, as well as prejudicial attitudes toward immigrants. In any event, a far more balanced viewpoint is needed—and positive psychology can help provide it.

For example, Dr. Fernando Ortiz (2017) of Gonzaga University observed that Maslow's concept of self-actualization is applicable to Latino culture but needs to be refined in accordance with its predominant values. In his view, these include *familismo, personalismo, simpatia,* and spirituality. In an everyday context, these terms refer to an emphasis on the family as a source of support, a preference for trustful connection with others, a cooperative interpersonal attitude, and a religious view of life. In addition, Latinos/as embrace an affiliative (rather than an individualistic) locus of control and self-concept as a primary cultural value. A study by Dr. Manica Ramos (2014) for *Child Trends* noted too that "Latina mothers support their children's education in ways that reflect Latino cultural values and beliefs . . . such as *sacrificios* (sacrifices), *consejos* (advice), and *apoyo* (moral support) . . . in ways that may be less apparent to teachers."

In this activity, interview two people who were raised by Latino/a immigrants to the United States; your interviewees themselves may have been born in the United States or elsewhere. Your questions may include these: In your view, how do Latino/a values about happiness differ from those of mainstream Anglo-American culture? For example, is happiness more related to family togetherness for Latino/as? Are celebrating religious holidays and events also more important for personal happiness? How about the definition of success? In your experience, do most Latino/as define it differently than do their Anglo-American counterparts? If so, how?

Record below the results of your interviews.

Your Work: **Please use this space, and additional journal space as appropriate, for your work.**

_____

_____

60 TOP THREE LESSONS

For the last activity, we would like you to write about the top three things you will take with you from this course or the specific experience of using this workbook. Because positive psychology is a very large scholarly umbrella, there are many research topics covered in any relevant overview of the field. In this workbook, there have been activities focused on positive emotions, life satisfaction, curiosity, nostalgia, flow, mindfulness, tears of joy, gratitude, a sense of wonder, emotional intelligence, positive relationships, and many more. We hope that you have enjoyed all the activities to some degree. At the same time, we recognize that no one responds to all the activities in the same way. Indeed, the theory of self-concordance states that the benefits derived from activities such as these, or any self-help interventions, are directly related to how well the activity fits with the individual's personality and life. If an activity fits and feels right for a person, then motivation is increased for both the initial practice of the activity and for its consistent practice over time. Fairly obviously, if an intervention feels right to us, then we are more motivated to continue it.

For this final activity, please write about the three activities that meant the most to you, the ones that best fit with your personality and life. If you wish, you can also write about three ideas, insights, epiphanies, or realizations that you will take with you. Write about how these three fit with your life, what made them relevant for who you are as a person and for your current life. Next, please write about how you will actualize, develop, or make them real in your life in the future. That is, *what will you do* from a *practical* standpoint to move from brief experiences, ideas, insights, or epiphanies toward making these a permanent part of your life? How will you maintain a consistent practice over time? Please be very specific and very concrete about this. For instance, rather than saying, "I'll remind myself to start meditating again," you should examine why you stopped meditating and implement a strategy to correct the source of the interruption to your meditation practice. Finally, write about at least one strategy you will use to get yourself back on track if your motivation fades and you stop trying to actualize your ideas. No one would be so naive as to suggest that changing old patterns in life and adopting new ways of living—even positive ones—will be simple and lacking any challenges. Therefore, when you "fall off the wagon" or lose your motivation, how will you get back on track?

Your Work: **Please use this space, and additional journal space as appropriate, for your work.**

_____

_____

_____

_____

REFERENCES

Adler, A. (1930). *The pattern of life*. New York, NY: Greenberg.

Adler, A. (1938). *Social interest: A challenge to mankind*. New York, NY: Greenberg.

Aldwin, C. M., Jeong, Y. J., Igarashi, H., Choun, S., & Spiro, A. (2014). Do hassles mediate between life events and mortality in older men? Longitudinal findings from the VA normative ageing study. *Experiential Gerontology, 59*, 74–80. doi:10.1016/j.exger.2014.06.019

Aristotle. (1908). Nicomachean ethics. In W. D. Ross (Ed.), *The works of Aristotle, 9.* Oxford, England: Clarendon Press.

Berman, M. G., Jonides, J., & Kaplan, S. (2008). The cognitive benefits of interacting with nature. *Psychological Science, 19*, 1207–1212.

Binder, M., & Freytag, A. (2013). Volunteering, subjective well-being and public policy. *Journal of Economic Psychology, 34*, 97–119. doi:10.1016/j.joep.2012.11.008

Bossard, J. H. S. (1944). The mental hygiene of owning a dog. *Mental Hygiene, 28*, 408–413.

Bryant, F. B., & Veroff, J. (2006). *Savoring: A new model for positive psychology*. New York, NY: Psychology Press.

Chang, P. J., & Yarnal, C. (2018). The effect of social support on resilience growth among women in the Red Hat society. *Journal of Positive Psychology, 13*(1). Retrieved from https://doi.org/10.1080/17439760.2017.1374442

Chen, Y., Mark, G., & Ali, S. (2014). Promoting positive affect through smartphone photography. *Psychology of Well-Being, 6*(8). doi:10.1186s/13612-0616-0044-4

Coulson, J. C. (2012). *Parents' subjective sense of calling in childrearing*. Unpublished doctoral dissertation, School of Psychology, University of Wollongong.

Csikszentmihalyi, M. (1997). *Finding flow: The psychology of engagement with everyday life*. New York, NY: Basic Books.

Dawkins, R. (1990). *The selfish gene*. New York, NY: Oxford University Press.

Duncan, L. G., Coatsworth, J. D., & Greenberg, M. T. (2009). A model of mindful parenting: Implications for parent-child relationships and prevention research. *Clinical Child and Family Review, 12*, 255–270. doi:10.1007/s10567-009-0046-3

Einstein, A. (1972). Letter of 1950. *New York Times*, March 29.

Enright, R. F. (2001). *Forgiveness is a choice: A step-by-step process for resolving anger and restoring hope*. Washington, DC: American Psychological Association.

Erikson, E. (1950). *Childhood and society*. New York, NY: Norton.

Filep, S. (2007). Flow, sightseeing, satisfaction and personal development: Exploring relationships via positive psychology. In *Proceedings of the 17th Annual CAUTHE Conference*.

Fredrickson, B. (2013). *Love 2.0: Creating happiness and health in moments of connection*. New York, NY: Plume.

Fredrickson, B., Cohn, M., Coffey, K., Pek, J., & Finkel, S. (2008). Open hearts build lives: Positive emotions, induced through loving-kindness meditation, build consequential personal resources. *Journal of Personality and Social Psychology, 95*(5), 1045–1062.

Fujiwara, D. (2013). *Museums and happiness: The value of participating in museums and the arts*. Presentation, Museum of East Anglian Life.

Gabhainn, S. C., & Sixsmith, J. (2006). Children photographing well-being: Facilitating participation in research. *Children & Society, 20*, 249–259. doi:10.1111/j.1099-0860.2005.00002.x

Gruber, M. J., Bernard D. G., & Charan, R. (2014). States of curiosity modulate hippocampus dependent learning via the dopaminergic circuit. *Neuron, 84*, 486–496.

Haidt, J. (2000). The positive emotion of elevation. *Prevention and Treatment*, 3(1), article ID3c. Retrieved from http://dx.doi.org/10.1037/1522-3736.3.1.33c

Hartig, T., Mitchell, R., De Vries, S., & Frumkin, H. (2014). Nature and health. *Annual Review of Public Health, 35*, 207–228.

Hartwell, D. G. (1996). *Age of wonders: Exploring the world of science fiction.* New York, NY: Tor.

Hoffman, E., & Acosta-Orozco, C. (2015). Life-metaphors among Colombian leadership students: Core values and educational implications. *College Student Journal, 49*, 438–446.

Hoffman, E., Neeta D. G., & González-Mujica, J. (2013). Tears of joy in India. *Indian Journal of Positive Psychology, 4*, 212–217.

Hoffman, J. (2015). The look of love is in the dog's eyes. *New York Times*, April 16.

Hutcherson, C. A., Seppala, E. M., & Gross, J. J. (2008). Loving-kindness meditation increases social connectedness. *Emotion, 8*(5), 720–724.

James, W. (1907). The energies of men. *Philosophical Review, 16*(1), 1–20. doi:10.2307/2177575

Jefferson, T. (1771). To Robert Skip with a list of books. *The Letters of Thomas Jefferson.* Yale Law School, Lillian Goldman Law Library.

Jia, L., Hirt, E. R., & Karpen, S. C. (2009). Lessons from a faraway land: The effect of spatial distance on creative cognition. *Journal of Experimental Social Psychology, 45*, 1127–1131.

Jourard, S. (1959). Healthy personality and self-disclosure. *Mental Hygiene, 43*, 499–507.

Kashdan, T. B. (2013). Curiosity protects against interpersonal aggression: Cross sectional, daily process, and behavioral evidence. *Journal of Personality, 81*, 87–102.

Kashdan, T. B., & Biswas-Diener, R. (2014). *The upside of your dark side: Why being your whole self—not just your "good" self—drives success and fulfillment.* New York, NY: Avery.

Kashdan, T. B., Rose, P., & Fincham, F. D. (2004). Curiosity and exploration: Facilitating positive subjective experiences and personal growth opportunities. *Journal of Personality, 82*, 291–305.

Kasser, T., & Sheldon, K. M. (2009). Time affluence as a path toward personal happiness and ethical business practice: Empirical evidence from four studies. *Journal of Business Ethics, 84*, 243–255.

King, M. L. (1967). *Where do we go from here: Chaos or community?* New York, NY: Harper & Row.

Lakoff, G., & Johnson, M. (1980). *Metaphors we live by.* Chicago, IL: University of Chicago Press.

Langer, E. J. (1989). *Mindfulness.* Reading, MA: Perseus.

Levinson, B. M. (1962). The dog as a "co-therapist." *Mental Hygiene, 46*, 59–65.

Logue, C., Hector, M., & Hutchens, T. A. (2005). Student leadership: A phenomenological exploration of postsecondary experiences. *Journal of College Student Development, 46*, 393–408. doi:10.1353/csd.2005.0039

Lyubomirsky, S., Tkach, C., & Sheldon, K. M. (2004). *Pursuing sustained happiness through random acts of kindness and counting one's blessings: Tests of two six-week interventions.* Unpublished manuscript, University of California at Riverside.

Maddux, W. W., & Galinsky, A. D. (2009). Cultural borders and mental barriers: The relationship between living abroad and creativity. *Journal of Personality and Social Psychology, 96*, 1047–1061.

Martínez-Martí, M., Hernández-Lloreda, M., & Avia, M. (2015). Appreciation of beauty and excellence: Relationship with personality, prosociality and well-being. *Journal of Happiness Studies, 17*(6), 2613–2634. http://dx.doi.org/10.1007/s10902-015-9709-6

McLean, K. C., Pasupathi, M., & Pals, J. L. (2007). Selves creating stories creating selves: A process model of self-development. *Personality and Social Psychology Review, 11*(3), 262–278.

Morrow-Howell, N. (2003). Effects of volunteering on the well-being of older adults. *Journals of Gerontology Series B: Psychological Sciences and Social Sciences, 58*, S137–S145.

Muir, John. (2014). *The Yosemite.* Charleston, SC: CreateSpace. (Original work published 1912)

Nagasawa, M., Mitsui, S., En, S., Ohtani, N., Ohta, M., Sakuma, Y., . . . Kikusui, T. (2015). Oxytocin-gaze positive loop and the coevolution of human dog bonds. *Science, 348*(6232), 333–336. doi:10.1126/science.1261022

Nakamura, J., & Csikszentmihalyi, M. (2009). Flow theory and research. In C. R. Snyder & S. Lopez (Eds.), *Oxford handbook of positive psychology* (2nd ed., pp. 195–206). New York, NY: Oxford University Press.

Nesteruk, O., & Garrison, M. E. B. (2009). An exploratory study of the relationship between family daily hassles and family coping and managing strategies. *Family and Consumer Science Research Journal, 34*, 140–152. doi:10.1177/1077727X05280667

Oritz, F. O. (2017). Self-actualization in the Latino/Hispanic culture. *Journal of Humanistic Psychology*. Retrieved from http://journals.sagepub.com/doi/10.1177/0022167817741785.

Parent, J., McKee, L. G., Mahon, J., & Foreh, R. (2016). The association of parent mindfulness with parenting and youth psychopathology across three developmental stages. *Journal of Abnormal Child Psychology, 44,* 191–202. doi:10.1007/s10802-015-9978-x

Perlow, L. A. (1999). The time famine: Toward a sociology of work time. *Administrative Science Quarterly, 44,* 57–81.

Peterson, C., & Park, N. (2009). Classifying and measuring strengths of character. In C. R. Snyder & S. Lopez (Eds.), *Oxford handbook of positive psychology* (2nd ed., pp. 25–34). New York, NY: Oxford University Press.

Proyer, R. T. (2013). The well-being of playful adults: Adult playfulness, subjective well-being, physical well-being, and the pursuit of enjoyable activities. *European Journal of Humour Research, 1,* 84–98. doi:10.7592/EJHR2013.1.1.proyer

Proyer, R. T. (2017). A multidisciplinary perspective on adult play and playfulness. *International Journal of Play, 6,* 241–243. doi:10.1080/21594937.2017.1384307

Ramos, M. (2014). The strengths of Latina mothers in supporting their children's education: A cultural perspective. *Child Trends Hispanic Institute.* Retrieved from https://www.childtrends.org/wp-content/uploads/2014/06/Strengths-of-Latinas-Mothers-formatted-6-10-14.pdf

Rollins, S. Z., Garrison, M. E. B., & Pierce, S. H. (2009). The Family Daily Hassles Inventory: A preliminary investigation of reliability and validity. *Family and Consumer Science Research Journal, 31,* 135–154. doi:10.1177/107772702237932

Roosevelt, E. (1960). *You learn by living.* New York, NY: Harper & Bros.

Salovey, P., Mayer, J., Caruso, D., & Yoo, S. H. (2009). The positive psychology of emotional intelligence. In C. R. Snyder & S. Lopez (Eds.), *Oxford handbook of positive psychology* (2nd ed., pp. 237–248). New York, NY: Oxford University Press.

Schiffrin, H., Edelman, A., Falkenstern, M., & Stewart, C. (2010). The associations between computer-mediated communication, relationships, and well-being. *Cyberpsychology, Behavior, and Social Networking, 13*(3), 299–306.

Schreier, H. M. C., Schonert-Reichl, K. A., & Chen, E. (2013). Effect of volunteering on risk factors for cardiovascular disease in adolescents: A randomized controlled trial. *JAMA Pediatrics, 167,* 327–332.

Seligman, M. E. P. (1991). *Learned optimism.* New York, NY: Knopf.

Seligman, M. E. P., Rashid, T., & Parks, A. C. (2006). Positive psychotherapy. *American Psychologist, 61*(8), 774–788.

Seligman, M. E. P., Steen, T., Park, N., & Peterson, C. (2005). Positive psychology progress: Empirical validation of interventions. *American Psychologist, 60,* 410–421. doi:10.1037/0003-066X.60.5.410

Shapiro, S. L., & Carlson, L. E. (2009). *The art and science of mindfulness: Integrating mindfulness into psychology and the helping professions.* Washington, DC: American Psychological Association.

Sheldon, K. M., & Lyubomirsky, S. (2006). How to increase and sustain positive emotion: The effects of expressing gratitude and visualizing best possible selves. *Journal of Positive Psychology, 1*(2), 73–82. doi:10.1080/17439760500510676

Stolberg, T. L. (2008). Understanding the approaches to the teaching of religious education of pre service primary teachers: The influence of religion-scientific frameworks. *Teaching and Teacher Education, 24,* 190–203.

Surtees, P. G., Wainwright, N. W. J., & Khaw, K. T. (2004). Obesity, confidant support and functional health: Cross-Sectional evidence from the EPIC-Norfolk cohort. *International Journal of Obesity and Related Metabolic Disorder, 28,* 748–758.

Thoits, P. A., & Hewitt, L. N. (2001). Volunteer work and well-being. *Journal of Health and Social Behavior, 42,* 115–131.

Turpyn, C. C., & Chaplin, T. M. (2016). Mindful parenting and parents' emotion expression: Effects on adolescent risk behaviors. *Mindfulness, 7,* 246–254. doi:10.1007/s12671-015-0440-5

USC News. (1994). *Remarks from USC's 111th commencement honorary doctorate recipients.* Retrieved from http://news.usc.edu/4824/REMARKS-FROM-USC-S-111TH-COMMENCEMENT-HONORARY-DOCTORATE-RECIPIENTS/

Vallerand, R. (2015). *The psychology of passion: A dualistic model.* New York, NY: Oxford University Press.

Ward, R. M., DiPaola, D. G., & Popson, H. C. (2009). College student leaders: Meet the alpha female. *Journal of Leadership Education, 7,* 100–118.

White, M. (1966). The camera mind and eye. In N. Lyons (Ed.), *Photographers on Photography*. Englewood Cliffs, NJ: Prentice Hall.

Wildschut, T., Sedikides, C., Arndt, J., & Routledge, C. (2006). Nostalgia: Content, triggers, functions. *Journal of Personality and Social Psychology, 91*(5), 975–993.

Zeki, S. (2007). *Statement on neuroesthetics*. Institute of Neuroesthetics. Retrieved from http://www.neuro esthetics.org/statement-on-neuroesthetics.php

Zhou, X., Sedikides, C., Wildschut, T., & Gao, D. G. (2008). Counteracting loneliness: On the restorative function of nostalgia. *Psychological Science, 19,* 1023–1029.

CPSIA information can be obtained
at www.ICGtesting.com
Printed in the USA
BVHW091311190722
642199BV00004B/82

9 781544 334295